An AffaiЯ Worth Remembering
With Huntington's Disease

Incurable Love & Intimacy

During an Incurable Illness

10th Anniversary Edition

An AffaiЯ Worth Remembering
With Huntington's Disease

Incurable Love & Intimacy

During an Incurable Illness

10th Anniversary Edition

Debbie Pausig

2024

www.Debbiepausigmft.com

First Printing: 2014

An AffaiЯ Worth Remembering With Huntington's Disease/Debbie Pausig
10th Anniversary Edition 2024
ISBN:979-8-9912212-1-4
EBook ISBN:979-8-9912212-3-8

Book Layout © 2017 BookDesignTemplates.com

THE TITLE

An affair: I picture a black-tie event where Sean Connery, as James Bond, exits his Aston Martin wearing one of his delicious tuxedos. Not so today, the media and society have us programmed to think and picture otherwise. The simple word "affair" brings to mind connotations and the sensationalism of illicit sex. And then come the questions, so many questions. Who is the affair with? Is it the other woman, the other man, the job? Who is involved? What is involved?

An affair drives a wedge into a relationship creating a triangle. When was the last time you heard of an illness driving a wedge between a couple or family members? Ali McGraw's illness in the fictional 1970 movie, "Love Story", with Ryan O'Neal comes to mind. Two young, married, mid twenty "somethings", deeply in love, whose lives are interrupted by a wedge named "cancer." Trying to "protect her", he attempted to keep her impending death a secret. She, of course, knew better. Their affair with cancer was brief. Their love, however, was not.

An illness, especially a progressive terminal illness, affects life, love and intimacy. An illness can take a family BEYOND normal chaos and dysfunction. The knowledge of an illness, its lack of knowledge, the illness as a "family secret", the unknown history of an illness, the timing of first symptoms in one's life cycle and a long debilitating progression, are factors that feed the fire of chaos and dysfunction. What trumps all is LOVE. I'm describing the type of love that evolves from young, feel good, sometimes hedonistic, lust and fascination, to a deep caring that spans decades. Deep caring love transcends the mind, body and soul. It is that kind of love for a person in times of turmoil and heartache that life with the illness is worth remembering. It is the kind of love that can endure experiencing the pain of change. It is the kind of love that learns to accept and include an affair with a disease and grow in the midst of it. It is the kind of love that remains after the illness has taken the "life" of the love, not the memory. It is the kind of love that leaves an imprint in the heart of the survivor where it is stored forever.

The "affair" I speak of here is an illness. This illness is Huntington's Disease. The word "AffairЯ" in the title is deliberately spelled with a capital and reverse facing "Я." R is for remembering. When I remember, I look back to the past, not remain in it. I am remembering that my "AffairЯ" with Huntington's Disease is worth Remembering. This is a story that involves incurable love and intimacy during an incurable illness. Powerful; *Yes.* Was it worth the risk of heartache and monumental hard work to maintain and survive; *Absolutely*! There was no cure for Huntington's Disease for us and there still is no cure. Scientific research is working on this life stripping, progressive, inherited, degenerative brain disorder. There was and is no cure for the kind of love that inspires this author and graces the pages of this book. That kind of love, my dear readers, is best left **incurable**.

COVER STORY

You have picked up this book and more than likely have noticed the title which I have already explained. Let's talk about the meaning behind the cover design. You probably think it is just a couple of random shapes connected in a rather sloppy manner. No my friends, it has a far deeper meaning than that. You see, LOVE is represented by the Hearts and the WEDGE is represented by the triangles. Are you following me? The illness, **HD** (Huntington's Disease), is the WEDGE. The 4 Hearts represent my husband, our two children and me. The 3 triangles bearing the letters "**HD**" represent my husband's 3 generational roles affected by HD: a son and brother in his family, a husband, and a father. And the shaky, loopy, uncontrollable and unpredictable string represents the journey that connected us with HD because it was all of that. As you read on you will find much more.

If HD was a "soup", some of its "ingredients" or symptoms would include those similar to ALS (Lou Gehrig's Disease), Alzheimer's Disease (ALS) and Parkinson's Disease OH MY!

CONTENTS

INTRODUCTION

10th Anniversary Note

Welcome to the 10th Anniversary Edition of "An AffaiЯ Worth Remembering With Huntington's Disease." There are a few changes to this book from the original published in 2014. You will learn that I am still grieving 16 years after Perrys death. I am learning more about self-publishing and hope this 10th Anniversary Edition is a bit more polished than the original. It is hard to believe that 10 years have passed since I took a chance and wrote this book. I am thrilled to announce I am releasing my second book, "The Freshman ~~15~~ 16 of Grief, Losing My Forever Love & Finding My Way." The Freshman ~~15~~ 16 begins at Perry's death in 2008 through the 16th death anniversary year in 2024. You can find a description at the end of this edition in the "Also, by Debbie Pausig" section.

Peace & Love,

Dedications

Perry

To my late husband Perry Pausig who was a kind, loving, gentle and selfless man. He was a husband and father; son and brother; uncle, nephew, friend and so much more. He lived life to its fullest as long as he could. He was a man who found the zest to live with the unknown that he might be the "**one**". The **one** of three offspring in his family that had a destiny of no one's asking. His destiny was to inherit the gene that robbed his own mother's ability to function for herself, with and for her family just seven years before I met her. His destiny was to be stricken with Huntington's Disease (HD). HD had affected the way he lived before the symptoms surfaced at age 33, the way he lived in the early stages after the diagnosis, and the way he lived during the middle and later stages. Perry died with the utmost dignity. Still giving of himself, he chose to donate his brain to scientific research. He hoped a cure would someday be found for this life stripping, progressive, inherited, degenerative brain disorder. This insidious family disease is called Huntington's Disease.

Family

To our parents, Ralph and the late Marcia Pausig and the late Katherine and John Kornitsky who were our role models in caring through sickness and health till death did they part. And, to your unimaginable strength and courage during the heartache and grief of witnessing one of your children perish from this disease. You are our heroes.

To our siblings and extended family who gave us their support and presence during this journey and loss.

And most lovingly to our children, Katherine and Daniel, who gave us life and the gift of parenthood. We love you so very much beyond spoken words. Our hardship was long and at times merciless. Yet, the love you gave to and received from your dad, and I was stronger and now timeless. My return to school, career reinvention and writing this book was a long and arduous journey. Yet, it was nothing compared to our journey with HD. Thank you for your support, understanding and patience. I am proud of the fine, caring and loving young adults you have grown to be. "I'll love you forever, I'll like you for always, as long as I'm living.........."

Friends

To the many angels I have been blessed with, during and after Perry's lifetime. You picked me up when I fell from emotional, physical and psychological fatigue. And when I fell again, you were there to pick me up and hold me. Through care packages, time-outs, hugs, simple presence, and a deeply appreciated, "How are YOU doing?" you exuded true friendship and love to us when it was needed so. Your continuous prayers throughout the struggles of our journey with HD and beyond have helped keep me going.

To my brothers and sisters in the North Haven, CT Police Department, I could have never balanced work and home without your watchful eyes on Perry when he was out in public. And, for your compassion and understanding the challenges I encountered with this disease.

My Educators and Colleagues

To my professors in the Marriage and Family Therapy Program at Southern Connecticut State University; especially Ed and Suzy; your knowledge, direction and education on family systems, structural family therapy and hierarchies helped me discover the deep effect an illness has on a family and its members.

To my many colleagues and peers "in and out" of the HD Community who have supported me during this writing. Your coaching, check-ups and check-ins have helped me stay on task as of late. This book has been slow cooking for 6.5 years. You helped me "turn up the heat" and it is now finally ready to be served.

Lastly, to Sr. Mauryeen, a very special mentor who introduced me to working with the bereaved shortly after Perry's death. This work has opened my eyes to see God's path for me and continues to give me the passion to see it through.

Thank you and may God Bless All of You.!

Notes:
This book is infused with current reflections, ramblings and musings. These reflections are italicized to note a brief off shoot or separation from the flow of the ongoing story. They are inserted in areas where relevant. These reflections are a result of my MFT, Trauma, Death, Dying and Bereavement Training as well as my current experiences as a therapist, bereavement facilitator, HD support group leader and my continued life as a widow of HD

Answering the Questions:
Why, Who and What?

Why am I writing this?

My intention is to capture the essence and meaning of "living" with Huntington's Disease as a spouse, partner, caregiver and adoptive parent. I want those who are living with and caring for those with HD to know that they are not alone. Much of what I write will normalize the two lives I lived with HD. I am referring to the life of love and the life of hell. I became a family systems trained marriage and family therapist (MFT) after my husband died. During my training, I not only learned how HD unbalanced my family system, I truly "understood" it because I lived it. I also want to capture the love we shared while he was trapped in that sickly vessel called the human body. He was not HD. HD did not define him. He had HD. He now "lives on", after death, through the memories recalled by each and every person he touched during his life. He lives on by the love that is kept in a special place in my heart. He lives on through the signs and ADC's (After Death Communications) I receive from him.

I have a life full of possibilities because of my late husband Perry and Huntington's Disease. I am a therapist who treats what I have lived through, a grief counselor, bereavement and caregiver support group facilitator. I understand the process of continuous grieving **during**, yes, **during**, an illness like Huntington's Disease and after. I am a spouse and caregiver survivor of

HD, and a HD widow turned therapist. Oh yes, if you are reading this book, I am now an author!

Who/What am I writing it for?

As a spouse survivor of HD, I am writing this for families, young couples, couples whose biological clock is ticking, and are living at risk or mildly symptomatic with HD.

I am writing this to increase awareness about HD.

I am writing this **not** only for those families at risk for or living with HD, but for other families that are enduring the trials and tribulations of a chronic, progressive or terminal illness whether short or long lived.

As a family systems trained therapist, I am writing this for my peer therapists, counselors, social workers, active and interning, educators of therapists, counselors and social workers who know that there are clients who will seek their help for illnesses that imbalance a family's system.

I am writing this as a woman, wife and widow who experienced what the power of LOVE **can** do in a relationship.

What will it do to make a difference?

This story validates and normalizes the frustration, resentment, craziness, chaos, sadness, anxiety, depression, dysfunction, burnout and heartache of living with a spouse who has HD. This story also remembers the depth of love that remained present throughout the illness. This is not just another love story. This is a story of how Huntington's Disease and Love influenced and changed a couple's and family's life.

This book is meant to be an inspiration. It is a book about hope, faith and perseverance. It's a book that explains the marriage vow of "until death do us part". It's a book ultimately about acceptance, acceptance of God's plan for us and, what we can do once we accept that plan.

I am shouting out to the therapists, counselors and social workers: Look at the family system! It's all about the system! Not a single "IP" lands in your office with sole symptoms. They are a symptom of dysfunction in their system. You may not be able to cure the organic illness affecting it. However, you can bring awareness of how the illness is affecting the family's balance. The "IP" in this story distracted my focus on the progression of HD.

Suzy, where is my mobile? Where are my stress monkeys? Picture a mobile with a family of four. Then put a monkey (a weight) on someone's back. That monkey represents a stressor that weighs a family member down causing the family to lose its normal balance and fluidity. Just imagine adding one monkey after another for each stressor. The mobile becomes so out of balance that there seems no chance of recovery. Everyone in that family is affected by the stressor monkey one way or another.

- 1 -

That Someone

He Was That Someone

Merriam Webster.com 2014 defines an affair as "a matter that concerns or involves someone".

He was a lively 20-year-old, a free spirit, and a jokester. He was that someone sitting across the banquet table ever so subtly brushing his finger from the corner of his mouth "into" his mouth. It was the nonverbal action that shouted, "Hey! You've got lettuce hanging out of your mouth and before anybody else sees it, I suggest you put it "in" where it belongs." "You look silly, really silly!" He was that someone who concealed the basket of rolls under the table just to order another one," for the table" because he liked bread.

He was that someone you meet again the first day of college on a sunny and warm September day. That someone you conversed with for 8 hours by the giant oak tree that cascaded shade over the cozy courtyard of the small university campus. He was that someone whose conversation carried on that same night, again by the oak tree whose cover now blocked the glow of the moonlight sky. Company and conversation provided the perfect distraction to an event gone awry. Dancing to a band in the student center came to a sudden dark and silent halt as the band's energy blew a fuse. He was that someone who captured your attention, like a schoolgirl. Yes, that 17 going on 18-year-old college freshman schoolgirl.

He was that someone who "mentioned" he had to have a nameless minor surgery. I thought it at least deserved a get-well card. He was that kind of someone who was well suited for a humorous card. That someone who was given a card with a pic-ture of a guy lifting the sheet in his hospital bed screaming YIKES!!!!! It showed his eyes bugged out like telescopes. One could only imagine what happened to the guy on the card. Ironically, that card was "spot on." He was that someone at the youthful age of 20 who just had a vasectomy. And, that minor surgery he mentioned was not so minor at all. It was certainly not minor in the description of its aftermath having left his scrotum razor burned, swollen, black and blue. The get-well card just might have been his reaction after all.

A VASECTOMY! Why did that someone choose to have one and at such a young age?

He was that someone who acted out of love and selflessness. This was something in the decades to follow I began to understand. He was that someone who was soon to be the special someone in my life. He was my first, the one that took my breath away. I mean "really" took my breath away, so much so that I hyperventilated the "first" time. How is that for a memorable moment?

He was tall, slender, and had an athletic build with long legs. He had short, dark blonde hair and blue eyes that sparkled like Caribbean blue topaz. And he had a smile that was equal parts mischief, coy and just plain cute.

He was that someone, who said he would marry a woman that could take care of herself in case something, happened to him. Did he find that woman? Yes, indeed he did. And she is lucky enough and blessed enough to tell his story through her eyes and heartfelt memories.

"He" was my friend, my partner, and my husband, Perry.

woman who walked with an intense stagger. It looked like a drunken stagger. Each step was exaggerated and wobbly, yet her movements were stiff. Her arms flailed as if she was often waving. Her speech was slurred yet understandable. If I had not known better, I would have thought she was drunk.

HD behaviors can be mistaken for drunkenness. The police may get involved for this very reason. There is little known by law enforcement agencies on how to approach and act with a person who has HD. The Huntington's Disease Society of America (HDSA) has a Law Enforcement Tool Kit available for training police agencies. Also available is a Caregiver Law Enforcement Tool Kit that helps HD families prepare for potential challenges with Law Enforcement due to HD related behaviors. It includes a Caregiver Guide, Crisis Template, Profile Card and an informative "I Have Huntington's Disease" wallet card. (www.hdsa.org)

Her hair was short, dark and wavy. There was something striking about her facial features. There was a photo nearby of her in her youth. She was the spitting image of Audrey Hepburn! An Audrey Hepburn doppelganger! She had a defining outer beauty. HD took away that youthful look and striking characteristics. As time went on, I learned what it did not take away. It did not take away her kind nature. Nor the kind loving look she had when her warm brown eyes made contact with mine. I will never forget that look. Those warm brown eyes had a deep loving look for her husband, Ralph. That look grew into a search for caring. It was a voiceless, please care for me because I can no longer care for myself, look. Perry had that same kind loving look in his later ye

-3-

He, We & HD

He + Me = We

Our relationship spanned three decades. Only through death did our marriage part after only 29 years. Perry and I married, never intending on having children. We were both college educated, worked full time, traveled and lived life to its fullest in our first decade. We were the typical "DINKS" (Double Income No Kids) of the 1980's, we were "twenty-something." "Time" so we thought, was on our side. We dreamt about retirement and our love for scuba diving was the key to our dream trip. We dreamt of going on a month-long holiday to Australia. Oh, how we planned this future that would be 40 years from our thoughts. At that time, we would be "only" sixty-something. We had it all figured out. First, we would rent a Winnebago RV, travel the continent and then finish by scuba diving on the Great Barrier Reef! IT was to be only a dream.

We + HD

So, where you may ask does the AffairЯ come into play? My biological clock was ticking. Actually, it did not tick. I was feeling the "gong" vibrations of a grandfather clock. It was the strike of Big Ben in London. It was a Carnegie Hall size Steinway Grand Piano falling from the sky onto my head. I was 33 years old; Perry was 35 and we had been married for 14 years when God sent that piano as my message to become a mom. We discussed it and, oh how the years had changed us. Perry wanted children to love and grow with him and ultimately, without him. He did not want me to be "alone" after he was gone.

What About the Big "V" at Age 20?

Remember the Title Page? Back in the fall of 1977 Perry had that "minor" surgical procedure called a vasectomy. It is considered a permanent method of birth control in men. Perry chose this procedure as a method to eliminate the possibility of passing on the HD gene from him to any future offspring. He did not know at age 20 he was gene positive. That scientific advancement came many years later. Perry started showing early symptoms of HD at age 33. Our suspicions were confirmed by neurological testing at age 35. (It was 1992. Science did not identify the mutated gene until 1993)

Plan "B" For Baby

The next logical step in baby making was artificial insemination using donor sperm. There lies the true difficulty in baby making. For a year and a half, we tried and tried and tried. For me, came the physical and emotional rollercoaster of infertility drugs, pills, needles, testing and IVF. Anyone who has ever experienced the emotional and physical boot camp of infertility may remember the bloating, 30 pounds of weight gain, crying, crying, the physical pain, vicious mood swings, anxiety and sadness, especially when it doesn't work. There was the mission to get to the appointments. Ovulation now is a precisely controlled and timed event. There is a small window period to get those guys in there to do their thing. Or, for the egg retrieval in IVF where a baker's dozen is the goal only to learn there are only 4 or 5 "good ones". The result was two failed IVF's and one miscarriage at 10 weeks. I could not go through it any more physically or emotionally. The irony of it all, Perry was sterile by choice, I was infertile by nature. The official diagnosis was undiagnosed infertility. I simply described myself as damaged goods. Who knew? We gave ourselves a reasonable timeline of 1½ years of infertility treatments before moving on.

There is a saying, when you plan, God laughs. After the infertility experience, I feel that we were trying to control a situation that was not in God's plan for us. He had a greater plan in store for us.

I am work in progress. Every time I try to control a situation, thinking it is the "right" thing to do, it backfires. When I "Let Go" and hand it over to God through faith and prayer it works out. I admit, I am stubborn and hail from such stock. I continue with the control and letting go struggle. My being a work in progress will be a life-long event, indeed.

-4-

The Success In Failure

A Second AffaiR

Just when you may think one affair is enough, especially when it involves a disease, ANOTHER comes about. Keeping with Merriam Webster, this is a matter that both concerns us and involves us and two other parties. These parties "to be" were not a wedge driven into our coupledom. These parties were a blessing, a new beginning, a new chapter in our book. These parties gave us life and we gave them life. We truly began and created a life together. These parties were unknown to our sight and mind. Yet, we had enough love, in our hearts and were open enough, to include them.

This second AffaiR started with the choice to become adoptive parents. *Our love AffaiR* was with our soon to be adopted children whoever they are and wherever they might be. This AffaiR also is spelled with a Capital "R". Because our journey, into parenthood and as parents under the umbrella of HD, is worth Remembering. Once again, it's all about LOVE. Yet, this

AffaiR's capital "R" is right facing. It is right facing because this is our future, and we are looking forward.

The Next Door Opens

I grew up in the Catholic Church and that is where we began the inquiry into and process of adoption. The lovely little nuns in my church were so excited to hear of our interest. Catholic Family Services had a meeting at a local church about international adoptions. The children were in orphanages in several Eastern European countries. We looked into the procedure for each country according to their laws. One country required travel to meet the children, leave them and come back in a month. Another required a stay of several weeks, a return to the States and back again for the children. And another required the prospective parents to travel to the country, meet the children and confirm the adoption. The entire "new family" would then return to the States. Guess which one was for us?

I could not imagine the thought of going to a country, meeting "our" children then leaving them behind. Nightmares of law changes, countries closing their doors to the international adoption process, or any other red tape made my head spin and heart pound.

Trusting The Process And Our Faith

There were a couple of potential challenges in the process. The first was getting a letter from Perry's Neurologist giving his professional opinion that Perry was healthy enough with early HD to enter into parenthood. Perry was at the early stages and very functional at the time. The application and the home study was another step. It was time-consuming and very thorough, as it should be. This is a serious matter involving the lives and welfare of children

The biggest challenge was the waiting game. We decided that we wanted two children, a boy and a girl. It did not matter whether they were related, and it didn't matter what ages they were. We knew we could only go through this process one time and one time only.

We started the process in January. Like many new parents-to-be we decorated the bedroom the kids would share. They were going to be small so two would be okay in one bedroom. Coming from the orphanage setting we thought they might find comfort being together. We took into consideration the culture shock from a non- English-speaking country to English speaking as well as the transition from one set of care givers to another. It would be an adjustment to say the least.

We painted a large blue, red and yellow, primary color rainbow that started from one wall corner and ended at the other. I felt like the rainbow represented our journey into parenthood. It began in our home and traveled to where the children were. We accessorized the room with baby Mickey and Minnie Mouse. The icing on the cake was a comfort piece. My grandfather's wooden rocking chair was the perfect addition to rock them calm or to sleep. It was worn on the arm rests from his years of use. I vowed to never refinish the chair because I wanted his character, his touch, his loving presence to remain on the worn finish. I wanted his quiet love to flow through me as I rocked my little ones in comfort.

Testing Our Faith In The Process

We received a call in October from the adoption attorney. She said she had a 9-month-old girl and an 18-month-old boy, non-related, available for adoption. We were delighted! All she could tell us was that they were healthy.

A second call a few days later slammed that door of joy in our faces. The little girl had taken ill, and the children were no longer available for adoption. Our hearts were ripped from our chests in disappointment and our hopes of being parents once again were shattered. All we could do to carry on was to close the door to that beautiful room we created with love for our new little loves.

It would be two months of trying to heal from the latest pain of disappointment. This had become another emotional roller-coaster on the journey to parenthood. We wondered how some people can have children so easily. How can some people have many children? Looking at the science of conception, it truly is a miracle that it even occurs at all. The sight of babies, toys, clothing, pregnant friends, baby showers and other parents with children was a constant reminder of something we couldn't have. Or could we?

8,730 Miles To Home

It was now December, and the holiday season was in full swing when we received the next phone call. It was the adoption attorney once again. She said she had great news! There were two children available. They were biological brother and sister. She was 3 ½ years old and he was 22 months. And, yes, they were very healthy. "There was just one thing", she said. My heart went from hopeful once again to a stifling dead silence. Do I dare trust again, have hope again? I listened. Her "one thing" was we had to act fast. Fast meant within one week's time, we had to make travel arrangements in lightning speed, we were going to Lithuania!

We traveled. And, the moment we laid eyes on "our" children, we knew they were perfect for us. She had Perry's hair color and my brown eyes. What was uncanny was her face was the exact shape of mine at that age of 3 ½. He was a spirited little tike. I'd say a blend of Perry and my younger brother.

In this getting to know you phase, we were instructed to take them back to our hotel which was an hour's cab ride away. Before we knew it one puked on my lap and then the other followed with projectile vomiting onto Perry's lap. To the best of my recollection, I think they emptied themselves of peas, potatoes and turkey.

We were officially christened into parenthood! In a few short days the adoption process was completed. We were parents, we were officially a FAMILY! And we named them Katherine and Daniel.

There was a light in Perry's eyes that I had never seen before. It was fresh and new. It was youthful and stress free. That light extended to his arms as he held both children. I captured that special light in a photo. That light embraced new life, hope and a future for all of us. It was the glow of a new Dad. That was the light of LOVE.

I had no clue what it would be like for all of us heading home. We were new parents with small children flying for the first time together. Air bound, we were crossing the Atlantic to their new home in the U.S. We landed at JFK Airport, cleared Immigration and were more than ready to go home. Connecticut was home for all of us.

Our first and most important stop was to be welcomed by our parents and new grandparents, Mom K. and Dad P. Dad captured the beautiful moment in a photo which showed equal parts joy and exhaustion on our faces.

As I reflect on that photo, it indeed looked like we returned from a very long journey. Yes, the journey to parenthood was certainly a long one. If love was measured in terms of wealth, we returned with greater wealth because the love in our hearts had increased exponentially.

It was an 8,730-mile round trip. Our family doubled in size in 4,365 miles

Joy To Our World!

Our new family was home, just in time for Christmas. Katherine and Daniel were "our" Christmas miracle!

Perry was a smitten and doting Dad. The look in his eyes as he held and played with "his" children was priceless. I think he carried so much love inside and was overjoyed to know that he did not pass the risk of HD onto them. He would carry them on his shoulders, let them climb all over him, and just purely enjoyed them. The sound of their laughter as they played with their dad was music to my ears. He was a wonderful Dad!

Perry was on top of the world when he took the kids fishing. That was his forever favorite past time, especially with his own Dad. He would take the kids across the street to a neighbor's pond or with Grampa on the boat. Eventually he passed the fishing torch with Grampa on to Daniel when he could no longer safely access the boat. We created a special ceremony to mark the torch's passing.

Perry would soon teach Katherine how to make pancakes and his special Butterscotch Chip pancakes. (*It's a secret recipe so don't dare ask.*) To this day, only she can make them as perfectly as he. Other traditions the kids remember that only "Dad" could do best are his grandmas German Egg Pancakes, and his own very famous Apple Crumb Pie. The kids insist NO ONE makes a pie like their dad, not even me. Grampa agrees, "Close but no cigar!" Perry left them his legacy and some great lifetime memories.

Traveling Memories

I promised Perry that as long as he could ride in the car, I would drive him. We did as much as we could for as long as we could. Short day trips throughout New England, driving to South Carolina, flying to Disney World, FL, California and Wisconsin are just a few. We went to local Dude Ranches and experienced as much quality family time as possible.

We made memories and took plenty of pictures. It would be in a few short years; that is all we would have, pictures and memories of a man enjoying life with his children. I took every photo opportunity that was possible. I wanted to and needed to capture the moments where the kids would someday see, how much their dad loved them and to be with them. *This was before the digital age. I probably should have bought stock in Kodak at the time. I should have bought stock in the film processing as well as there were always double prints made for sharing.*

It is funny, when I think back to the photos I saw of Perry as a kid, he usually made faces during the picture taking process. Not so as a dad. The smiles on all their faces were simply PRICE-LESS!!

There were few photos of me because I was the one behind the camera. I wanted to make sure those "Kodak" moments were being captured.

The Calm Before The Storm

It would be a couple of years before HD progressed to the point where Perry could no longer work. He started forgetting little things. The Chorea part of HD was affecting his fine motor skills. That gradually progressed to his gross motor skills, and he began walking with a staggering gait just as his mother did when I first met her. We still functioned as normal a family as we could. The progression of HD was documented at our annual appointment with our neurologist.

Other little things were happening. I saw obsessive-compulsive type behaviors occurring. Perry loved to fish. Back in the day, he would place a catalog order from L.L. Bean or Cabela's by check and mail or telephone credit card. His obsession rang through when he "needed" his fishing gear and ordered "overnight" delivery. He did not "need" the gear for several months. His brain with HD, needed it "now". And if that was not soon enough, he would drive to a nearby Super K Mart that was open 24 hours because he "needed" a package of fishhooks for the weekend or later. Perry's disappearing in the middle of the night for fishhooks became another HD stressor on me.

- 5 -

....

The Long-Rocky Road

"Driving" Me Crazee

There are so many things we take for granted like mobility and the ability to drive. It was a challenge to say the least when it was not safe for Perry to drive a car. He was also an avid motorcyclist. He drove a used BMW touring bike. We joked about owning a BMW but could only afford 2 wheels. He drove that motorcycle everywhere he could. He once took it to a motorcycle rally in Wisconsin with a friend. On Sundays, he would go for a 4-hour ride through back roads in Connecticut. He would section off the map and tackle a section each week. It broke his heart when he saw it necessary to sell the bike. He wanted to make sure he sold it to someone who loved riding as much as he did. When that right person came around, it was sold. He gave up the bike before he gave up driving a car.

Perry was getting into minor motor vehicle accidents which made my stress level soar. Over our three decades, he had gotten into numerous accidents; some were his fault, some were not. It was only when HD was obvious that I started to take serious notice and do something about it.

I thought then that it was the chorea that made his driving bad. As I have learned recently, it may have been the cognitive impairment which occurs long before chorea may surface that was the culprit.

We had him professionally tested to assess his driving ability and doggone it, he passed! I was angry and I was scared to death. He mustered all he could to concentrate and pass. That may have been all well and fine for that brief assessment. It was not okay with me knowing that every time he went for a drive, he could potentially get hurt or hurt another. I was terrified each time he went out behind the wheel that it would be his last time.

Sadly, I had to pull rank and pleaded with his neurologist for safety-sake, Perry's, his family's and others. It had gotten to the point where it was just not safe for him to be behind the wheel. A compassionate man, his neurologist did tell him that the HD had progressed to the stage where it was not safe to drive. Perry accepted the doctor's order.

Guardians In Blue, Watch Over Thee

Now unable to drive, Perry took to walking around town. He would walk to give blood at the local blood drives. I think he was a member of the "10 gallon" club. Always thinking of others, he knew he could help with a blood donation. He thought, after all, his blood was not affected by the HD. He would also walk to the local track and help out the local high school track team train as he had done years before. He had always been an athlete. He was a high school and college pole-vaulter on the track and field teams.

Wherever he walked in town, he had guardians watching over his back. I was a police officer in the town where we lived. Perry was also an officer in the same town for a short while before he moved on. The "PD" as I will refer to them was great! They were our "Guardian Angels in Blue". I will never forget how they cast a "blue blanket" over Perry. When I was working and some of my brother officers saw Perry walking in town, they would give me a "heads up" to his location. At that time Perry walked with a staggering gait.

We were fortunate because they knew he had this neurological disease called HD. There was never a question of public drunkenness or inappropriate behavior. He was as gentle as a lamb. He had the disposition of a golden retriever not an attack dog. Generally, I knew where he was headed by the location he was spotted. My PD had "my" back. They were a great group of men and women to work with. I was blessed.

2001 Accidental Fallout

Pedal power was Perry's next mode of travel when he could no longer drive his motorcycle or car. He would bicycle, run, or walk. He was always active.

Perry had an inner drive to keep going. I envision a voice that drove him. The voice said, "You can't run away from me, I'm HD", "You can't run away from me, I'm HD!" It was the voice of HD.

He had a few bicycle accidents. One resulted in 56 stitches in his face. Now I've seen my share of blood in my time but watching him get stitched up took my stomach over the edge. I remember walking out of his area in the ER to "go to the bathroom". I felt white as a ghost and ready to hurl whatever was in my gut. There is something about seeing an innocent loved one in distress because when they hurt, we hurt. Thank God he always wore a helmet.

In October 2001, he had an accident that would be the end all be all of his activity as he and I knew it. I will never forget; I was working at the time. I was told that Perry was in a bicycle accident, and it was a serious one just a few streets away from home. He was riding his bike on the right side of the road and turned left in front of a tow truck that was traveling in the same direction. Hearing those few details, I knew it was going to be a bad one.

By the grace of God once again, Perry's head was saved by wearing his helmet. His left hip and leg were not so lucky. He required emergency surgery for his trauma resulting in screws securing his left hip and a rod in his leg. The post-op x-ray looked like someone had thrown a handful of sticks in him from the "Pick-Up Sticks" game we played as children.

He was in intensive care for 2 weeks. I took the midnight shift by his bedside during that time. My mom was living with us and had the kids covered for care. I tried juggling work and the bedside shifts, but I just couldn't and had to take some time off. Perry then spent a month in a local therapeutic rehabilitation center that strengthened him enough so he could come home.

Little did I know that I was about to enter a whole new ball game with HD. In this one, the players included caregiving struggles, family friction, and a boatload of emotions. The emotional toll and fallout had just begun. The toll to pay was a high price.

"MY" Perspective: Good Times Turned BUGLY

Every family member could write their own story from their own perspective. And every story would be recorded differently. There is no one way of telling this story. There is no wrong way of telling this story. There is no right way of telling this story, this is what I recall. And, with this perspective, I take ownership of my words. I own up to both my strengths and shortcomings. I did the best I could at the time with the resources I had. BUGLY is my description of Bad and Ugly.

I have learned from my continuing education in Family Systems Therapy, Grief Counseling and Death Education that my story is in the realm of normal, whatever normal is.

That accident changed things, at least in my mind, for the remainder of Perry's life. I had come to be a comfortable member of my in-law's family from our beginning in 1977. This accident made me feel like an "outlaw" rather than an in-law.

It started at the hospital waiting room after Perry was admitted. He was awaiting emergency trauma surgery, and I was devastated and in shock from the events that had just occurred. Though in emotional shock, I had to make decisions. I was head of our household. We had 2 kids, and they were only 10 and 8 years old. They did not know what was going on with their dad. They had to know that their dad was not coming home that night. I did not know what the immediate future held. All I knew was he was in bad shape. My father-in-law and his wife arrived along with the rest of Perry's family. I needed support yet felt so alone. I did not feel supported or comforted. *Looking back, I now understand they too were in shock and frightened.*

The reality of Huntington's Disease reared its ugly head like a mythical dragon emerging from a dark cave. It found its time to come out of the cold and ugly darkness; its wrath began.

My mom had the kids covered. Yet, I had to be mindful of her limitations. Just 2 years earlier she had undergone a double mastectomy for breast cancer and chemotherapy treatment. Now at age 72, her cancer journey was continuing as well.

We all reacted differently and in my own grief and shock, I was protective of Perry and defensive of my actions. My actions were love and fear driven. I called my best friend Debbie who quickly came to my side. There was nothing to do but wait.

WAIT!!!!! I was a person of action, I needed to DO SOME-THING!!

I managed to get in to see Perry just before surgery. Thankfully he was conscious and alert. I needed to know what he, my husband, the father of our children, wanted me to do. I would follow only his wishes. I asked if he wanted me to stay and wait out the surgery or go home and take care of the kids. Both of us knew it would be hours before he was out of surgery and recovery. By that time it would be early morning. He said, "Go home and take care of the kids". I respected his wishes and did just that. His family was appalled that I would leave him at this time of need. I tried explaining that it was his request that I leave at that time. Both Perry and I knew it would be hours before I could see him again. He, having loved his children so, knew that I had to tell them what happened. And they needed their Mom to deliver such a message. News like that threatens their security in the family.

A Time When Security Was Already Shaken

Keep in mind that this occurred only one month after the 911 attack on New York's World Trade Center (09-11-01). The nation's sense of security had already been shaken. As parents, we had to ensure security within our own family unit. We had to comfort our children and assure them that their family nucleus was safe. They had to know and feel that everyone in their household was okay including Dad, Mom & Babcia (Grandma). And, thankfully, the rest of our family was safe.

Perry was in the hospital for about 2 weeks and once stabilized he was moved to a local rehabilitation hospital where he spent about a month. The kids and I would stop at a local fish market on Friday nights and have fried shrimp (his and all our favorite) family dinner in the dining room. The hospital even allowed us to bring a pet. We had two cats, and we brought Perry's favorite, Tubby.

Tubby is a beautiful domestic short hair cat. He is jet black with sage colored eyes. There was something special about Tubby. Perry was generally not fond of cats. Tubby changed that. He was only a little over a year old at the time and he had great intuition. He was our guardian angel. He walked around the hospital bed to check out the room then sat and settled on Perry in normal comfort as if he was at home. *At 14 years old today, he remains our guardian angel cat, supervisor of those who visit and keeper of the flock.*

Action Mode For Me

While Perry was in rehab, I continued to run with an energy level that was akin to a bee collecting pollen from flower to flower. I was on a mission; a mission to work my job; a mission to care for my children; a mission to visit my husband in rehab on a regular basis; and a mission to prepare for his homecoming.

In preparation for that homecoming, I used exhaustive resources to get a hospital bed into our home. We prepared a bedroom on our main and level floor. I went to Tag Sales and found gently used durable medical equipment at affordable prices. In came a basic wheelchair, a commode, and a shower chair. His sister and husband purchased an electric lift recliner. His room was ready for a comfortable, loving and thankful homecoming.

Was I Hearing Things?

One day Dad and I were visiting Perry at the rehab hospital. The two of us walked to an outdoor sitting area. He asked me if this was a contest in who could take better care of their spouse. I didn't quite understand the statement. I do not even know how I responded. I do remember being shocked to the core by the question. My head was ready to explode from the stress of what was happening already. I was already in over my head with the weight of all the responsibilities in the present and what was to come. I started questioning myself, was I doing enough? I thought my intentions were love based, honorable and protective of Perry.

I did not know what was going through Dad's mind at the time. I can't imagine having to experience this horrible disease with one's own child. He had already been through this once with his late wife, Perry's mom. *I can only picture the scars left behind as a surviving spouse and caregiver after witnessing my beloved's battle with HD because I too carry those scars. I cannot imagine what it was like for him carrying the burden that each of his children was at-risk of having HD. Nor the burden of knowing one of my children has it as was in Perry's case. And the burden knowing what Perry's certain future was with this disease that has no cure.*

I picture that constant worry likened to a Chinese water torture. Every minute of every day of every year it is a slow drip on the skin. Each drop is an unforgiving reminder of the disease's presence. It might be distracted by work, activities, or vacation. It might be out of sight; it is never out of mind.

I cannot imagine what a parent like my father-in-law lived with every day. Only in recent years I had glimpses described to me. One friend is currently bookended by HD. Her husband is currently in the advanced stages and her 14-year-old daughter has Juvenile HD. Another acquaintance lost her husband to HD and recently lost her 24-year-old daughter to Juvenile HD. A woman I just met lost her husband and two children. She said in regard to research, "It is too late for my family!" I have no words to describe what these parents and families are experiencing.

The man that I looked up to as my own Dad was questioning my motives and my intentions. I was hurt, I was confused, and again, I felt alone. I thought we were in this together. When I married Perry, I married the family. I married Huntington's Disease. I did not think the fallout from this wretched illness was going to cast a light on me as a "bad person", the evil one, the outsider, or the "outlaw". I was afraid, afraid that I would not be a "good wife" if I didn't do what I could for my love. All that mattered to me was caring for my husband and my children. It didn't matter so much that I neglected myself.

I remember fondly how everyone, all of us adult kids and spouses, rallied around Dad when he was the caregiver-spouse with Mom P. I was hoping that I would receive the same type of support. The difference was we were adult children giving support to our parents. This was a different relational situation because I was hoping for moral support from his family. Our children were too young to give me that kind of support. It was not their position to do that because I was the parent and adult. At the time they were still young children.

I now see that my expectations from my in-laws were just that, "my expectations". In my own grieving process during this stage of HD, my sadness, helplessness, anger and frustration were being projected onto his family. My mind wanted them to circle the wagons around "me", the caregiver and the loving wife. My unmet expectations left me feeling abandoned by the whole family.

The very people I needed love and support from, Perry's family, were not available. Time would reveal this was the beginning of my slide down the slippery slope of despair. It was the start of a slow and steady 2 year out of control spiral.

Out of fear, nerves and a general sense of survival, I continued to "do" stuff. I called out for help from my brother police officers. We needed a way to get Perry into the house. A couple of fellows came to my aid and built a ramp. It was a beautiful sturdy ramp that would last the rest of his life enabling him easy access in and out of our home.

Homecoming came just in time for Thanksgiving 2001. It was the most thankful time I could remember in recent history. We celebrated Thanksgiving and his homecoming at our home sweet home. It was a simple and very memorable one as his sister and her husband joined us. We even wheeled Perry across the street to our neighbor's pond which was a favorite fishing spot of his and Daniel's. It was pure quality family time.

In-Home Help Hurts And Hurdles

Perry needed help with in-home care giving. His Dad and his wife stepped in and arranged for her sister to come in for a time. Having a family member to help take care of him seemed a perfect solution. We all got along and enjoyed having her around.

We soon experienced hurdles. She lived about 30 miles away and encountered car troubles and traffic delays. I needed to get to work in the morning. The kids went to school. The stress of Perry not having coverage as I left for work became a sore subject. It was a difficult discussion with a family that was already so generous with help.

Eventually, the family member could no longer help care for Perry. That weighed down an already strained relationship. We were now caregiver-less and in search of desperately needed help.

Where & How To Find An In-Home Caregiver

One thing I was not prepared to do was to search and interview Homecare Agencies for in-home caregivers. I did locate one in town. It was run by a woman named Jackie. Jackie was a loving and caring person who had an intense passion for this kind of work. She and her office assistant were able to find us a wonderful woman to come in and take care of Perry while I was at work. She gave such attention to detail and had a lively spirit. Jackie's home care agency had my back. If our regular lady could not come in, she made darn sure there would be someone at the house for Perry. That gave me great peace of mind.

When Help Has To Leave

I recall becoming heartbroken one day when our lady said that she was leaving Jackie's agency to pursue another job with higher pay. She had spoiled us with her care. Of course, I knew she had to go because that was best for her. Unfortunately for us, the emotional toll of the caregiver search had just begun. Then Jackie found another lady who was pretty good.

The bottom dropped out again when Jackie announced that her agency was closing. The search was on to find an agency that could provide us regular help for the long term. After what seemed like endless telephone calls and interviews, we did locate another agency.

When Hired Help Doesn't Arrive

The rollercoaster of hourly caregivers in and out was just that, a rollercoaster. Sometimes they came, sometimes not.

I could not understand the problem. Perry was not a behavioral problem. He had the personality of a golden retriever, not an attack dog. He needed help with the basic needs, washing, toileting, dressing, and feeding. And, if the weather was nice, they would take him for a walk around the block. He needed assistance with walking and was not wheelchair bound yet. There was no high-tech maintenance needed for my man with HD. So, what was the problem? My guess is the work ethic has changed. Some people come to work and just want to be present and do the minimum. It seemed like they were just a step above companion. Anything "more" than that is just too much. The passion in caring for someone was just not there.

Then there was the mismatch. I recall one young woman came in to care for Perry as a last minute "fill-in". She was no more than 5' tall and 100 lbs. soaking wet at best. I thought to myself, how is she going to assist this 6'3", 185-pound man in the shower and toilet? I'm only 5'3" and had a difficult time. It was a 4-hour job and luckily didn't require much handling.

When The SH*T Hits The Fan

I think this heading tells it all. One morning I got dressed for work in my normal business attire as I was working as a

Detective. My shift started at 8 and I usually got in the PD by 7:30. Not that day. Just as I was ready to walk out the door, I heard Perry's voice calling "Debbie" from the bathroom. My poor helpless husband was standing above the toilet with his shorts down to his ankles. He was struggling with the toilet paper as he was trying to wipe himself. He was trying to be independent and do it all by himself without assistance because we didn't have coverage.

All I could see was smeared shit all over him, all over the toilet seat, all over the walls, all over the sink and the floor and him. Everywhere he touched as he struggled to clean himself was a mess.

I stood there and cried. I was dressed in good clothes. Not house clothes prepared for cleaning. My gut ached as I saw my Honey struggling to help himself. I quickly called my boss and explained the situation. Once again, my guardians at the PD had my back. He told me to get in to work as soon as I could.

I did what I needed to do. I cleaned up my Honey and got him settled. Then I cleaned up the bathroom top to bottom. It was not the way I envisioned the start of my workday. When I get to work, the shit can hit the fan. I was not ready for it to happen at home.

When Your Children Step Up To The Plate

It was heart wrenching to me when the kids at ages 10 and 8 had to step up to the plate to briefly cover care for their dad. On the positive side, I worked a mere 1.5 miles and 3 minutes away from home. The negative was when we didn't have caregiver coverage, and the kids had just gotten home from school.

I recall phoning home saying I was going to be a little late. I had to pick up a few things at the market for dinner. At this point, I'm only one mile from home. I vividly remember Katherine's voice say, "Don't worry Mom, I've got it covered." A river of tears rolled down my cheeks as I drove to the grocery. I thought to myself, why does a child have to be burdened with such a task? She was ready to care for her dad, whatever it took. Daniel stepped up as well. At 8 years old, he became a master at keeping company with his dad. They would watch fishing shows together on the television. They had it all under control.

2003 Anniversary Party

"Why don't you and Dad get married again so WE can be in the wedding?"

Even when we struggle, we look for the good things to remember. Perry and I used to joke about being married "3" times. We were first married by a Justice of the Peace. The second time was a formal blessing in the Catholic Church. The third time was on a tourist pirate ship in the Caribbean. There became a new meaning to "walk the plank mate". One would think, by the third time, I really wanted to be and stay married to this man. Or I just couldn't get it right, so we kept trying a different way each time.

It was 2003 and the year of our 25th wedding anniversary. Daniel was a new altar server at church. As we talked about the upcoming anniversary, the kids suggested, "Why don't you and Dad get married again so WE can be in the wedding? What a GREAT idea! And, with that idea, our minds began brainstorming the "perfect" wedding with the kids.

We had an August ceremony in our back yard. It was the perfect setting. It was also so appropriate for us because when we got married the "2nd" time, our reception was a picnic in my Grandparent's & Uncle's back yard including a dip in the pool. We wanted this occasion at our home, which was already complete with a swimming pool and plenty of room for guests. The theme was a Hawaiian Wedding ceremony.

Planning this event was exciting. I wanted to make this event the most memorable ever. I wanted it to be something that the kids would remember years down the road and reflect back on with a joyous heart. Guests brought food in lieu of presents. The guest list was a manageable 25 or so. Aloha to all.

The Bride, me; Maid of Honor, Katherine; and Best Man, Daniel, were donned with grass skirts. The Groom, Perry, wore one of his favorite Hawaiian shirts. We all wore special leis. Keep in mind, the grass skirt would have been too dangerous for him to wear with the unsteadied chorea walk. Daniel officiated at the ceremony because he was an Altar Server. He even read the vows which went something like, "Mommy, do you love Daddy, Daddy, do you love Mommy, okay, Group Hug!" And that is what the four of us did. We hugged and were so proud to get married again, for the "fourth time". The 4th time was the charm because our kids were in the wedding. If we were counting bases, we hit a home run with this ceremony!

It was an event to remember with our closest family and friends in attendance. We had great company and great food. It was a perfect event and commemoration of our 25 years of marriage. And of course, there were plenty of photos to help us remember.

When The Caregiver Crashes & Burns

Something I did not mention that between the 2001 accident through the beautiful Hawaiian Wedding celebration was the added toll it took on me. I was hell bent on making memories with Perry and the kids. And those memories were going to be positive.

I wanted the good memories of their dad to overshadow the difficulties. I was caught up in a vortex that I could not break away from. Then one day in October 2003 it happened.

I woke up one morning in a fetal position on my couch. I could not move. I felt despondent. Somehow, I mustered up enough energy to call myself sick to work. How I managed is beyond me. I felt like I was in a frozen state. I was in that state for 2 days when something in me knew that I had to do something. There were too many responsibilities at home with the kids and Perry. Thank God Mom lived with us because she had my back. I will never be able to imagine what she thought as she watched me. *(Nor will I ever know because she died 2 years after Perry.)*

Somehow by the grace of God, I managed to get to my Primary Care Physician who would not let me leave his office until I got help. He diagnosed me with an acute onset of Major Depressive Disorder as a result of Caregiver Syndrome. In simple terms, I was suffering from Caregiver Burnout. He set me up with a therapist and a medication manager. I needed the combination of talk therapy and medication for depression and anxiety. My brain was depleted of the natural hormones and ability to cope with what was happening in my life. Once again, HD reared its massive and ugly self and finally knocked me down where I could not get up.

This was a state that I never want to be in again. It was frightening. It took weeks and months to find the right antidepressant to stabilize me because everyone's body chemistry is different.

Talk therapy helped because I had to get out my thoughts and feelings of helplessness. No one could fix my problem (HD) as it was going to progressively get worse. The therapist had an unbiased ear to talk to. I always kept my feelings to myself and did not vent to others. Hell, I couldn't even cry in public or in front of others. The situation was not going to get better. There was no hope for Perry's recovery from this disease. HD is a fatal disease, there is no cure. I was gradually losing him as this disease progressed and stripped him of who he once was.

I was numb. I could not laugh, and I could not cry. I was a flat lined heart monitor. There was a nothingness inside of me. I felt nonexistent. I do not know how I was able to function, yet I managed. If there was ever an autopilot in humans, my switch was in the on position. God was watching over me.

I felt extra fragile around my family. I recall that first Thanksgiving after I crashed. Perry, the kids, Mom and I went to Perry's sister's house for dinner. I drove there but I could not sit at the table. I recall retreating to their spare bedroom where I curled up in a bed and shook from severe anxiety. I couldn't face anyone, I couldn't socialize. I felt so frail and still so alone.

That following Christmas Eve, it was similar with my own family on Mom's side. We traditionally celebrated it at our house. Normally, I cooked ethnic food, and the family would bring their special dishes. I had nothing in me to "perform" that year. I remember my Aunt Ellen say to me, "Don't worry, what matters is that we are all together." They were the kindest and most understanding words. They were what I needed to hear. My family is not one for words. They show their love by their presence. The whole gang was present that Christmas Eve, making me feel included and loved.

It took the longest time for me to get my spirit back. I would say nearly 4 years to fully recover. I would leave the house when I needed to for work or other necessary things. It was so hard to socialize. I felt like I was behind a locked door. Though I held the key, I could not turn it in the lock and open it. I was afraid to open it and allow people to "see" me the way I was. It was a struggle every day. I needed to separate myself from the outside world and people.

So, what kept me going? My LOVE for my husband and my children kept me going. I was a wife and a mother. I had responsibilities. If it was not for them, I would have probably gone unnoticed and still be on my couch in that fetal position. Throughout his whole ordeal with HD, Perry and the kids were my medicine. They were my purpose in life.

I was grieving and was fighting it at least since the 2001 accident if not before. I was grieving the relationship that I had with Perry that was forever changing. I was grieving us as a couple, he as my partner, and we as functional parents. It was all on me. I had to be the breadwinner, man of the house, father and mother to the kids. Was I a martyr; I do not know. All I know is that I was drowning and over my head and I finally crashed and burned. I have always had a hard time asking for help. Much like my mom, I kept what is going on inside my house private. It was to my detriment, not asking for help. The straw finally broke this camel's back.

Caregiver, Patient or Both?

You would think the stresses of caregiving were enough by now, not by a long shot. Between August 2004 and March 2007, I had undergone 7 surgeries including 2 first rib removals, 2 carpel tunnel, 1 right shoulder procedure and 2 right shoulder joint replacement procedures. Of all the surgeries, physically, the first was the worst. I had the surgical removal of my right first rib due to scar tissue compressing the nerve causing numbness in my right jaw and arm. This scar tissue had built up from years of work-related shoulder injuries, re-injuries and surgeries. A serious complication occurred as my diaphragm became temporarily paralyzed causing my right lung to collapse. I, the caregiver, was now a patient.

Breathing was a problem. I was operating on only one lung. I tired easily. Simple moving about the house was weakening. It took 6 months for me to get full lung capacity back. Things that occurred during the early weeks after my surgery few people witnessed or knew about. Hired help was in and out during their "shifts". Mom had the kids covered as well as she could. My physical and emotional stress and strain occurred; you guessed it, off shift.

Home from surgery, I slept on a futon couch on the first floor in my office next to Perry's bedroom. I did not have the strength to climb the stairs up to my bedroom.

Perry was semi-mobile. He toddled some around the main floor of the house with assistance. He did need assistance. Without assistance, he would bounce from wall to wall when moving down the hallway. He would grab onto doorways as best as he could and fall when there was nothing to support him. He knew I was in bad shape and tried his best to move only when absolutely necessary. There were times when he just needed help and no one but I was around.

Running half empty with one lung, I could barely help myself let alone help Perry. I remember one day he was in the bathroom and needed assistance with toileting. One's bodily functions do not run in sync with the home health aide's schedule. He called out to me. I literally crawled out from my office futon.

Remember the "I've fallen, and I can't get up Ad on TV?" Yes, that was me except I didn't fall. I just did not have the strength to get up and walk. I inched along the floor on my belly crying and crying. I must have looked like one of those wounded gun slingers from the shootout at the O K Coral dragging themselves away from the Earp brothers and Doc Holiday. I probably looked like a wounded crocodile as it slowly slithers and limps away from an attack zone. I was so weak, and my Honey needed me. I called out to God, Help Me! Give Me Strength!

I was given that strength to do what I had to do, help my husband as he struggled with HD, and I struggled beside him. Help him to do yet another thing we "normal and functioning" human beings take for granted. I helped him wipe his ass. That is what we do for our loved ones. When they need us, we take care of them because we want to. Not out of obligation, out of love because love has no obligations.

Had I known then I was going to write a book, I would have taken better notes. Relying on mere memory is a bit challenging. Therefore, I am intentionally keeping some of these war stories with HD brief.

Goodbye PD, Hello ....

A HUGE change and yet another loss in my life occurred when my shoulder injury forced me to retire from the PD. I had to say goodbye to a 25-year career and the brother and sisterhood where I spent my entire adult life. My shoulder was done forever in police work. What I had to look forward to was a shoulder joint replacement. I tolerated the surgeries and new accommodations I had to make in my life.

Along this journey of surgeries and recuperation, I found an unexpected gift. This gift was something to be so special that I am forever grateful to have experienced it. I found the gift of time.

This was not just any old time; it was the time I was able to spend with Perry during the end of his time on this earth. We had time to wheel him and sit outside on our patio and enjoy the water fountain and fresh air. We had time to sit next to each other, arm to arm, and watch a movie. We had time to hold hands. I learned that this gift of time was more precious than anything I could imagine. This time allowed me to look into what were once sparkling and mischievous blue eyes now turning distant and empty. This time allowed me to learn how to read his body language because he lost the ability to speak. Time allowed me to learn to read his mind for his needs.

2005 Team Hope Walk

We sponsored the first HD Team Hope Walk in our town in October 2005. Our goal was to raise awareness in the community about HD. The Walk was my first real introduction into fundraising. Our community came together. We were well supported by friends, family and the community including the North Haven Police Department and the Girl and Boy Scout troops which Katherine and Daniel were members of.

The HD Team Hope walks continue today. They are bigger and farther than our 2005 one. It is wonderful to see how they have progressed.

I learned a very valuable lesson at the time of our HD Team Hope Walk. I am not a good fundraiser. I have difficulty "asking" for money. I hate asking for money. I have difficulty "asking" because I am a doer. It is no wonder why I burned out from exhaustion a few years earlier. I did not ask for help. I had to be independent as a child and that carried over into adulthood. No wonder why I met Perry's qualification in being a woman who could take care of herself in case something happened to him. In my mind, strong independent women don't need help. Boy was I wrong! I am getting better at asking for help. The resistance is deep inside me. It might even be in my DNA. This too will be a continuous growth process for me. Isn't it interesting that many of the people most willing to help are those least likely to ask for it. We cause ourselves so much suffering because there are plenty of people that are happy to help, if only asked.

Tipping Out Of Balance

Perry's accident in October 2001 was the beginning of what I call my official charge into single parenthood. I relied upon my mom to oversee the kids' activities and rides. I also did what most parents do when they need help. I looked to my oldest child. Katherine was 10 at the time of the accident and 13 at the time of my collapsed lung. I leaned on her and depended on her for various things to help me out. She had grown to be a trusting and capable adolescent. She was capable of cleaning the house as well as I and minding her brother. She looked after her dad when necessary. She was the "big" sister. She was very good at taking charge of things, one of those things being her little brother. She became a co-parent by default. It was a role Perry could no longer actively fill to help me oversee and run the house. It was also a role that caused complications. For the sake of survival, Katherine became a parentified child.

In family therapy the "parentified child" is one which is moved in the family hierarchy from the child subsystem to the parent subsystem. It is a place the child does not belong. That movement causes an imbalance in the whole family dynamics.

It took a few years in the making until our family system mobile was no longer able to self-adjust. It lost its fluidity. One member in particular became the sacrificial lamb, Daniel. It was November 2005 and Daniel was 12 going on 13 when we encountered behavioral problems. These problems were beyond the normal middle school early teenage stuff of dysfunction and chaos. "I" didn't get it.

What I did do is everything I could to get him the help he needed and ultimately, the help we as a family needed. Our family's house of cards was collapsing! I left no stone unturned. I sought out as many resources that were available to us and got into various programs to help us along this journey.

I recall one very young therapist that did not seem to "get it". She focused only on Daniel's behavior even though I clearly explained the circumstances at home with his dad's illness.

This is one of the reasons I became a family systems trained therapist. We needed family therapy. We were all struggling and suffering with the effects HD had on our family. I did not know that parentifying my daughter would have an adverse reaction with my son. The therapists he saw only focused on his behavior without looking and treating the bigger picture. Individual and family therapy may have helped; however, it wasn't even an option.

Dan had helped for many years. Interestingly, he and we all began recovering after Perry's death in 2008. Dan looks back at those years and the process he went through with disdain. I remind him that if he had not gone through the process, he may not have grown to be the fine, loving man he is today. He learned coping skills that will be in his toolbox for a lifetime. He gained wisdom from the school of life.

I look back at the heartache of watching my son suffer. I do not even know what was going on in Katherine's, Perry's or Mom's minds. All I knew was I was on the "front line" and I had to save my son.

In retrospect, I think Daniel saved me through his trials and tribulations. The energy that was put into making sure he would be ok was a distraction from Perry's continued progression with HD.

-6-

Voiceless Not Choiceless

A Dad Without A Voice Is Still Present

HD had taken away Perry's ability to speak. It was a gradual change. He once talked. Then he slurred. Then he garbled. Then he grunted. When he was adamant about something he was able to muster a strained YESSS or NOOO. Then it was looks and stares.

It broke my heart to think that someday I might not hear his gentle voice again or recognize his voice. All I can remember now was his struggled ability to say "Yes", "No" and "Debbie" as he called out during caregiving. It strained him so to even say his children's names. It brings tears to my eyes to think I might forget his voice. The thought of forgetting what his normal voice sounded like frightened me for a time.

He may have lost his voice and words. He did not lose what was left of his ability to be a father and to be part of our household.

One day Katherine brought a school friend over to the house, his name was Sean. They came in the house and walked by Perry who was sitting on the living room sofa. All of a sudden Perry started screaming!

Around 2007 more changes with HD were occurring. Screaming was one of those changes.

I sat with Perry and went through a bunch of questions that he was able to answer with a grunted yes or no. We finally came to the conclusion that Perry did not know who Sean was. And no boy, he didn't know, was going to be in our house with "his" little girl.

I brought Katherine and Sean back to Perry and formally introduced Sean to him as Katherine's school friend. Perry was fine after that. It was the most beautiful act of fatherly love. Even in his limited state, Perry was protective of and wanted to be included in his daughter's life. Though he no longer had a voice, he was present for his family.

The screaming was probably one of the last symptoms with HD that told my gut his time was running out. Perry had a couple of screaming spells that sounded like someone was pouring hot oil on him. It was blood curling and gut wrenching. They came out of nowhere as he sat on his favorite sofa. He did not complain of pain. It seemed as if something in his brain was misfiring or dying off causing this behavior.

- 7 -

What About Sex?

This is NOT "Fifty Shades of Gray"

The only shades of gray here are the hairs on Perry's and my scalps. Something happens in a relationship when one can no longer "perform". It goes deep, real deep. I did not think I needed sex because so many other things overshadowed my needs.

The obvious one was that HD progressed to the point that it just could not happen. Adult diapers, catheters, etc. Nope, those days were over. Another was I was just too darn tired. I was burned out and recuperating. I had no desire, even to service myself! *My kids are going to have a field day with that line.* My own libido was a no go. I soon learned in illness, there was a greater act than the coupling of two bodies. I am referring to the coupling of two souls.

The intensity of love and intimacy of our souls burned on. It smoldered longer and brighter than any night between the sheets. How can this happen? You might ask. Read on, Read on. ….

Intimacy At A Level Never Imagined

I loved Perry's mind, body, and soul. "I trust you" was expressed in his eyes when his lips could no longer form the words to speak. We experienced a level of intimacy few couples do because of the disease. My unconditional love for him continued to grow stronger throughout all the stages of HD.

When an intimate sexual relationship was no longer possible, the relationship deepened. I looked into his eyes as I spoon fed him making sure he did not choke. I held his hand and sat next to him feeling the energy of his presence. There was an intimacy I hadn't felt in our youth. Our youth brought us activities, conversation, partnership and the world. The disease took away our activities and our conversation. The disease did not take away our partnership; it opened up discovery to our inner world. It was a greater sense of being with each other. It taught us that there was an unconditional level of trust between us. It was an, "I will take care of you" till the end of time trust. It was an, "I will take care of you till the end of your time on earth" trust. And I did, till the end of his time.

Have you ever experienced unconditional love and trust with a pet? I have that same kind of unconditional love and trust with my cats, Tubby included. I unconditionally love them and they love me.

In both instances, there are no words. There is sight, some sounds, and undeniable presence.

This, my dear readers, is what I mean about incurable love and intimacy during an incurable illness.

- 8 -

Grieving Alongside HD

Caregiver Tunnel Vision

All I saw during my caregiving days with HD were the changes of people around us. I started to resent these changes. Family, friends and acquaintances seemed different. What I did not realize was that others were grieving the changes with Perry from afar. The kids and I were in the fox hole, we were living on the front line, every day 24/7 we lived, ate and breathed what HD was doing to our family.

One thing I did not see was how HD had changed "me". Perhaps people not only stayed away because of the changes the disease brought upon Perry, maybe it was the changes they saw in me. The friends and family that were a constant during the illness are a constant now. Did they understand what was happening to me? Have they forgiven me due to the circumstances?

I realize now that loved ones like Perry's dad, brother and sister were also grieving. It took a long time for me to learn about this grieving process. There was so much anticipatory grief with HD. The pain of seeing someone you love and care about change every time you visit them can be unbearable. The natural thing to do is to distance oneself to avoid the exposure and the pain of change. I felt abandoned by some when it was their own anxiety and discomfort that kept them away. I understand that now. If you are reading this book, I forgive you. Please forgive me for the resentment I felt during this perceived abandonment.

- 9 -

....

Grieving "During "The Illness

So Many Unexpected Losses

My first thought of "loss" is the actual death. And there are secondary losses that occur as a result of a death.

With HD, I experienced so many secondary losses before Perry's death. Strange as it may sound, it's as if the progression of HD prepared me for the losses after death.

In her book, The New Day Journal, Sr. Mauryeen O'Brien O.P. illustrates 19 "secondary losses" that occur after the loss of a loved one. Here I name the losses that occurred during our life with HD. These losses were experienced individually, as a couple and as a family. Let's see how many you too have experienced with HD, your chronic, progressive or terminal illness. I bet we have a lot in common.

Loss of a Large Part of Ourselves The part that we gave each other in a special way was lost. We lost the mutual physical bonding during sexual intimacy. He lost his ability to be mischievous and playful to HD. I lost my free spirit and playfulness to the stresses of caregiving. He lost his kind and gentle voice that spoke to me and the kids.

Loss of Identity We lost who we were as a couple. We lost our partnership in elbow-to-elbow activities and projects. I lost my lover. We lost the ability to do things as a couple. I lost my witness to life's moments that we shared as a couple.

Loss of Self Confidence I felt inadequate at times that I wasn't doing enough for him. I lost pride in caring for myself.

Loss of a Chosen Lifestyle We lost our ability to enjoy life spontaneously. He lost the ability to teach the kids the activities he loved.

Loss of Family Structure Here is the biggie as I have explained earlier in the book. Our family system changed with HD and the loss of Perry's parenting abilities. It tipped and lost its balance which created havoc within the family. I ran our household in single parent mode while the other parent is still present yet not able to function as such because of HD.

Loss of the Past As HD progressed and Perry was no longer able to communicate, we lost our ability to reminisce. He could no longer tell his silly tall tales only the way "he" could. When hearing a story of our "yesteryear" he could only muster a garbled yes.

Loss of the Future This one really needs no explanation. As HD's late stages progressed, we knew the kids would not have their dad present for proms, graduations, college move-ins, all events big and small.

Loss of Direction With HD's late stage progression surviving day to day was all that mattered. There was no direction.

Loss of Dreams With HD, we did not see our retirement years together. The dream of a retirement trip was our youth's fantasy.

Loss of Trust This came with depending on others for caregiving, visits and help. There were many broken promises. The late arrivals and no-shows of paid caregivers strained my trust.

Loss of Focus With HD and I imagine any chronic, progressive or terminal illness, caregiver exhaustion blurs everything. My focus on self-care certainly took a back seat. I even forgot to pay bills!

Loss of Control During the various stages of HD's progression, we had no clue what was going to happen next. It wasn't if something was going to happen, it was "when?" When was he going to fall? When was the next accident? When is the paid help going to arrive? When will our family get a breather? When can I take a break?

Loss of Humor Happiness, Joy As with my depression from caregiver burnout, I flat lined. It was almost impossible to feel anything, let alone anything upbeat.

Loss of Patience with Self I thought I was superwoman. I thought I could take care of my family. Boy was I wrong. I wasn't super anything. What I forgot was that I was a "human" with limitations. I had no patience or kindness for my own perceived shortcomings.

Loss of Health I had compromised mental health. Depression and anxiety were a result of caregiver burnout. Thankfully, with the assistance of a caring primary care physician, psychotherapy and medication, I fully recovered.

Lonely and Displaced

I was grieving who I was. I was Perry's wife and partner. I was also his caregiver. Caregiving did to me what the whale did to Jonah. It swallowed me up and took away Debbie the person and Debbie the wife. It left me feeling lonely and alone, neither of which were by choice. I did not have the strength to be both. I did not think I had the support to be both, so I chose the role that would serve Perry the best.

I also felt displaced. I felt like I did not belong anywhere. With Perry's family, I felt like "the caregiver", no longer an in-law or family member. I felt like I did not matter. I resented this yet allowed it to happen to me. I lost myself. I was empty and without purpose and direction.

-10-

The Power Of Prayer

Malnourished

I admit it, I am human. And as a mere human being in today's
world, life got busy. Living with and caring for a loved one with
HD was at times like battling a force of nature. It was the dense
fog making it difficult to navigate life's seas. It was the desert
sandstorm. Any chance of living with clarity was painfully pelted
with reminders that the journey was going to be a difficult one.
The journey was leaving me lonely and displaced, and I was without nourishment. Without nourishment, survival was proving to
be much more difficult.

Soul Food

The nourishment I needed was spiritual. I had gotten so caught
up in the vortex called "life with HD" my spiritual tank was running on empty. I needed to pull over somewhere at a rest stop

and refuel. Where and when had eluded me for quite a while. Until....

Until that major loss and change occurred. It was the closing of my lifelong career door, my retirement from the police department. My disabled shoulder opened not one but two doors at the time. The obvious one was the gift of time I received to "be" with Perry until his death. The second one occurred rather naturally as I had to slow down and convalesce from the surgeries.

The second door that opened was to my inner being and spiritual awakening. This too became a great gift. It was through prayers, reflection and giving thanks for what I had that made me stronger from the inside out. My inner healing process had begun.

As I continue to ground myself in the reminder to "Let Go and Let God", I feel relief in accepting what I cannot change. My spiritual tank is refueled and running at a normal level.

- 1 1 -

Running Out Of Time

2007, The Year Of Lasts

Our last hired caregiver was a live in. I had just completed the last procedure of my shoulder joint replacement. Perry was full service 24/7 care as we had graduated awhile back to Depends adult diapers, catheterization and many daily bottles of Boost or Ensure to maintain a high caloric intake and healthy weight.

Fifty Was Nifty

Perry's last birthday ever to be celebrated was his 50th in April 2007. We brought the party to him. What would be a unique "50" salute? A "50" balloon, balloon pit was created and scattered around the living room floor. We sat Perry in the middle of them all. He looked like a "Big" kid in a children's ball pit at a McDonald's play land. Our 4-year-old nephew certainly enjoyed joining him by jumping in. It was a "digital age" Kodak moment this time.

A Last Hoorah!

Of all the things we had done in our lives there was something we did not do. This was something that we still could do with HD. My last birthday gift to Perry was to lease a convertible sports car. We leased a Mazda Miata. Mazda's jingle is Zoom Zoom and "Zoom" we did. It was the most affordable sports car and it was a "gas" to drive and ride; it was peppy and fun.

The summer of 2007 would be our last to take drives. With the Miata, we drove and we drove. We would wheel Perry up to the car, load him in on top of a seat protector, drape a drool cloth on his shoulder, add a favorite ball cap, buckle him up and we would GO! I mean Zoom!

He always enjoyed the outdoors and driving with the top down was the best we could do. I added a long scarf to my head with a floppy rimmed sun hat and we cruised as if we were in an old British Racing Green MG circa 1960's.

Our summer drives in the Miata would last only a few hours each time out. I did not have the capabilities to change him if he soiled himself. It became our weekly "date" as weather permitted. After all, there is only one way to ride in a convertible, with the top down, of course. The fresh air, sunshine and freedom from captivity in the wheelchair and confines of home were just the right medicine for both of us. He usually nodded off and fell asleep during the trip. This was a sure sign he was relaxed. This was "our time" together. It was all the quality time we had left. This provided memories to "last" my lifetime.

Screaming, I'm Not Dreaming

I knew changes were happening and they were not good. Nothing that happened with the progression of HD was good. I spoke earlier about the screaming. This began happening with regularity. I thought more of his brain cells were dying from the HD progression and they were misfiring, but I did not know. There were no answers in the medical community.

Perry would be sitting on the couch and let out a blood curling scream. It was as if someone was pouring hot oil over his body. He had this terrified look in his eyes as the scream discharged every last bit of air from his lungs. He would sit up, tense up and let it out. Only after it was done, would he collapse back into the couch from sheer exhaustion. This screaming not only terrified him, but it also scared the daylight out of me. I felt so helpless. It pained me so to see him suffering. There was nothing I could do but watch. It looked like he was trying to release a demon. Might that demon be HD?

Upon hearing these screaming episodes, the kids sought refuge in their rooms. They wouldn't come out until a calm silence was restored. I can't imagine how frightening and painful it was for them. This unknown thing called HD was continuing to rob them of the father they knew. These episodes were changing the gentle soul they knew and loved. Though it was a small percentage of time that they occurred, they were unpredictable, fast and furious causing a lasting impression. It's been 7 years since I've heard that screaming and see how I was able to describe them so vividly.

Time To Prepare

By October 2007, my gut was telling me it was time to make some preparations. I went to our local funeral home to begin arrangements for Perry's final journey. The owners knew us and of Perry's illness. My heart hated the thought of our story coming to an end. My practical brain knew it was time to prepare. Had HD been preparing me all along for what I now had to do?

Heartfelt Pain Like No Other

Churning inside of me was the move to take the next step. It was December 2007 and time to look into the resources our local hospice had to offer for end-of-life care. My younger brother and I went to the Connecticut Hospice in Branford, CT. While inquiring, I felt the sharpest pain in my heart. It was as piercing as a precisely sharpened ice pick. Somehow my heart knew our journey with HD would end here. It was the pain of my heart breaking. The piercing pain fractured our beautiful time piece. My heart, while whole, had the workings of a fine watch made with Swiss movement. From that time on my heart was substandard. It was barely holding on as if my fine Swiss watch had been replaced with a cheap "knock-off" bought on some city street.

We qualified for in home hospice care until the end of January 2008 when Perry was transferred to inpatient hospice. The move to inpatient proved to be the final leg of the HD journey.

Forever The Captain Of "His" Vessel

I had a feeling that once Perry left home whatever strength and fortitude that was left inside him would take over. And it did. Once he was transferred to hospice Perry stopped eating. Thankfully, he was never in any pain with HD. Any pain he experienced was usually the result of injury from one of his accidents. He took in moisture from a sponge tipped stick. We had little time left and were able to have one last...................................

My Last Valentine
"True Love" is neither Physical nor Romantic.
"True Love" is An Acceptance,
Of all that is,
Has been,
Will be,
And will not be...
Author Unknown

Truer words could not be spoken as I encircled this poem around a picture of Perry and me for my last Valentine to him. I put it near his bed within his sightline and added the Hawaiian Lei he wore at our 25th wedding anniversary party.

As we visited, I even climbed into bed with him to watch a movie. Laptop computers are a handy device to prop onto a bed tray table.

A Son's Birthday Forever Changed

It was Daniel's 15th Birthday when I got the 3:00 PM call from hospice. They said that it would be a good time to return because Perry's body was showing signs of shutting down. Daniel and Katherine had just gotten home from school a short time earlier. We barely had time to acknowledge his birthday with some cake. Mom, Katherine and I sang Happy Birthday to Daniel. I explained that I had to go see their dad. His time was nearing its end.

Perry's sister and husband, my younger brother, and a few of our closest available friends joined us for one last gathering around our almost lifeless loved one. We talked, laughed and reminisced about his antics over the years. Hospice had provided us a special area where we were able to gather privately.

Our family and friends left, and it was just Perry and me in that room. It was so quiet that I could have heard a pin drop. Perry's body was still as he quietly breathed. His body was shutting down as I looked at his mottled legs under the bed sheet. The nurses said that his core was taking blood from his extremities. I sat in a chair by his bedside. It was still Daniel's birthday, and I "ordered" Perry NOT to die on our son's birthday! That would haunt our boy for the rest of his life.

Goodbye My Love

God Bless Him, he listened! One last nagging and it worked! The stroke of midnight and it was now February 27th. Still seated, I was craning my body over his. It was not a good position to rest let alone sleep. Then I thought, "He is NOT going to spend his last night on this earth alone!" I decided to shimmy his body over in bed just enough so I could sleep with him, one last time.

I had heard somewhere that though unconscious; people can still hear. I also heard that sometimes people need permission to die. I had also heard that people somehow wait for the right moment to die. Obviously, I had "heard" a lot of things. With Perry, they rang true.

It rained all night into the day. God was sharing our tears of sadness. Morning came and the nurses cleaned Perry up. As he lay motionless, breathing erratically, I stroked his full head of blonde and graying hair with my fingers.

HD had transformed the man I once knew. His once tall slender athletic built body was now tall and skinny with atrophied muscles. Muscles that once graced his arms, shoulders and neck had dissolved. All that remained were boney structures jutting from the cheeks in his face, collarbone, hips, knees and ankles covered with pale tissue thin skin. No longer could I see the eyes that sparkled like Caribbean blue topaz. His smile was no longer able to express that coy mischievous boyishness I once knew. The affectless mouth was a barely functioning opening allowing for inhalation and exhalation.

I wondered what he would look like if he was able to normally and gracefully grow into middle age. You may think this is silly. I think he would have looked a lot like Mark Harmon as Leroy Jethro Gibbs on NCIS! He would have had that lovely graying hair, those beautiful sparkling eyes and that smile. He was a bit quiet like Gibbs too. And from what I read about Mark Harmon, a bit of a jokester.

I gently caressed his face with my hands while I wept. I knew by his breathing that his time was nearing its end. I whispered softly to him that it was okay for him to go. We had a good life together. He was a good husband and Dad. I told him that I loved him so very much. As hard as it was, I knew it was the right thing for me to do. But he was not ready yet. He waited.......

He waited for his dad and older brother to arrive and joined me by his bedside. He needed to be near and hear his family just one last time. The night before, he was near and heard his sister. Now he was near and hearing his dad and brother; he was complete.

Perry was positioned on his left side facing me. He had to be on his side to prevent choking on his saliva and for drainage. I was able to stroke his hair with my right hand and his face with my left. Dad was to my right close to Perry's entire head. His brother sat directly across from me. He was able to rub the back of Perry's head and back.

We sat in silence. We wept in silence while we listened. We listened as his breathing became labored. We listened to the deafening silence between his few last breaths. I can only describe how focused I was on him, his face and my sorrow as he continued to slip away from this earthly realm. We heard "one last breath" at 1:18 PM on February 27, 2008. The man we all loved, the man we sat vigil over was no longer. Dad put his arm around me and said, "It's over now." We hugged. I was so thankful to have them with me at this critical moment. I will never forget that neither of us (Perry nor I) was physically alone during his last hours and moments. We were not alone spiritually either; God had gently taken Perry home to be reunited with his mother. *Uncontrollable tears are streaming down my face as I type this as if it was yesterday.*

It was now a critical period. Perry had decided to donate his brain to science. In order to preserve the brain, the nurses put a huge bag of ice under his head. The funeral home had been contacted to transport Perry to a local hospital morgue as soon as possible to remove the brain for transport to Mass General where it would be studied as his mother's was.

A Spiritual Transition

As I kept vigil over Perry's dead body, I adorned it with the Anniversary Hawaiian Lei from his room. I then witnessed something I'd only seen as special effects in a movie. I saw a golden shimmer rise from his chest area and dissipate upward into the air. I had a strong feeling that Perry's spirit had just left the vessel we call the human body.

When I looked back at his body, it resembled any other dead body I had ever seen. There was a "dead body look" I've seen as pale skin, eyes partially open and mouth partially open from the last breath. It is a "look I've seen before where the ill has died."

Please remember that I have seen dead bodies during my career in police work.

My heart and soul were convinced that Perry's essence, his spirit left his body at that time. It had been trapped in that sickly human vessel for too long. For the first time in "many" years, his spirit was FREE!! Free to be! Free to Soar! Free of HD!!!

Perry's body was picked up by the funeral home. I walked to my car and cried. As I cried, I noticed that it had stopped raining. I gazed at the western sky through my tear swollen eyes and saw the beginnings of a beautiful sunset. God was reassuring me that Perry's spirit was free.

A Special Place In The Sky Called Heaven

As I lay in bed the evening of Perry's death, I stared out my bedroom window. In the clear dark sapphire evening sky, I saw the biggest and brightest twinkling star in the southeast. He was giving me a sign that he made it to Heaven. Now, he was okay.

I talk to that star quite often. It has moved but is still very present for me. For the heck of it, I Googled, "What is the bright star in the southeastern sky?" Googles response was the planet "Jupiter". Though his body is no longer in my presence, Perry's spirit continues to soar. I feel it and sometimes see it. And it gives me great comfort.

"Perhaps they are not stars,

But rather openings in heaven

Where the love of our lost ones

Pours through and shines down upon us

To let us know they are happy."

Eskimo Proverb quote

-12-

I've Learned

Things I've learned during my HD journey and beyond...

I've learned patience. By not being in a rush to get to work or in the rat race to get anywhere, I've been able to spend more time with Perry. That time has been more quality time. I don't feel like I'm neglecting him, and I know he feels better about having me around for his needs.

I've learned to be more caring._ Perry's needs, for example, spoon feeding, requires my attention. I have been able to give him my undivided and loving attention. The kids are fully capable of feeding him when necessary because they have seen the type of interaction I have with him. Perry also knows I am just a call away with his toileting needs. I seem to hear him from anywhere in the house when the faint voice "Debbie" is called out.

I've learned to be calmer. I am no longer worried about Perry as I used to be. His days of wandering are over. My fears of him getting into bicycle or car accidents are over.

I've learned acceptance. Perry has weakened as he cannot walk the lengths, he used to nor exercise like he used to. I accept this and try to keep him safe in his own environment.

I've learned time is a gift. With everything this disease has taken away from us, I've found that TIME became a gift and gave us a second chance.

In taking the time for me to talk and listen to his one-word answers, I've learned that Perry does understand. He does respond, he does remember. I see it by the response in his eyes; his eyes smile and twinkle. I see it in his smile, that cute boyish smile I fell in love with. I've recently brought up his "relentless" sense of humor. He responded by smiling and turning red. The sight of him remembering specifics from the past warmed the depth of my heart and made my eyes tear.

I've learned not to be judgmental of others. As I have walked in no one else's shoes other than my own, no one has walked in mine. Therefore, I am not to judge other people's situations, and no one should judge mine.

Everyone's journey with HD is different, every person with HD, every family with HD. No one knows what went on in our lives because they were not walking side by side, eating, sleeping, breathing with us, 24/7, on this journey. There were few windows and doors open to that world. Because of pride, and the way I was reared, sharing and exposure was on a "need to know" basis. I grew up keeping what happened in our household closed to the outer world, family and friends included. The true level of suffering lies within each individual who lived under our roof. As we each are different, our perspectives of events are different as well. It is easy to be a "Monday morning quarterback, or critical Charlie" when you are not sinking in the quicksand or having to react on the front line." If I was ever asked, "Did you do your best at the time given your resources?" I would answer a strong YES from the bottom of my heart into the depth of my soul! What I did was out of LOVE.

I've learned I have but one regret. The biggest regret I have is not asking for help earlier and along the way. As I explained in an earlier chapter, I thought I could do it all. Not so! I am sure there were many hands willing to help, we needed only to ask. By failing to ask, I failed myself.

I've learned from other HD families. I have met so many beautiful people with HD and their families. Through my support groups, the conference, the convention and Facebook to name a few, I see that I am not alone in the emotions I experienced. I guess I am normal after all. They are my continued inspiration in the writing of this book.

And finally, I've learned…God chose Perry and I to carry the burden of this disease for he knew our love was strong enough to weather it. He knew we would be able to teach strong relationship values to our children by living what they've learned. He knew I would not leave, abandon or turn my back on Perry. He knew we would make this situation work for us instead of against us. He knew there were others out there we could help. He knew Perry was a fighter who agreed to bring HD Awareness to our area by a Proclamation from the First Selectman in our town naming May 2005 as Huntington's Disease Awareness Month. He knew Perry would be present at our first area HD Team Hope Walk in October 2005. Without Perry's agreement to any of this, I would not have proceeded. God has also chosen me as a conduit to help others through this book.

- 1 3 -

Life After HD…

Grieving Now In A Different Way

I thought all the losses I encountered during the journey with HD had prepared me for the end. In a way it did because I was continuously losing the person I once knew and had grown into mid adulthood with.

Grief after death I found was different. I think the most significant loss after this long journey with HD is the loss of presence. I miss his "being" if that makes any sense. I miss him being home; being available to listen to my babbling even though he cannot converse in return; being able to look at me and seeing that he loves me; being on the sofa, holding hands, arm touching arm and watching TV together.

PTHDCSD

Nowadays there seems to be an acronym for everything, Stores: CVS, BJ'S, H&M, etc.; Media: ABC, NBC, BBC, CBS, ESPN, HGTV, etc.; Cars: BMW, GMC, MB, MG, RR, etc.; Banks: TD, BoA, etc.; Clinical Diagnoses: OCD, PTSD, PMS, "HD" and even for comments: TGIF, LOL, TMI, IDK, and OMG. I think you have the picture.

I thought, there has to be an acronym for life after caregiving with HD. So, I made this up, PTHDCSD which translates into Post Traumatic Huntington's Disease Caregiver Stress Disorder. Post, because it's after the fact. Traumatic, because the many changes we experience with our loved one during the progressive journey with HD are emotionally distressing or disturbing. HD, Huntington's Disease of course. Caregiver, because that's who we were, caregivers of our loved one's mind, body and soul. Stress, because it is never ending. And Disorder, because that is what life with HD does to our family system. It creates a state of disorder and chaos. It disrupts our family's normal system of functioning. Just to clarify, I made this acronym up. You will not find it in the DSM-IV or DSM-V. (*See? Two more acronyms.*)

I usually do not diagnose myself. But somehow, I managed to fit into the criteria of this disorder. I knew I had it and am slowly working through it. And thankfully I am getting better. The intensity of caregiving my husband with HD plus the other things going on in life drained me of the liveliness and spirit I once had.

Even my father-in-law once mentioned that I had lost that liveliness.

The layers of losses that we experienced during my husband's last 7 years stripped me down beyond nakedness. The weight of each stacked layer became heavier and heavier to carry. The person, even I once knew, was socially and emotionally reduced. I was the animal carcass picked away by vultures. It stripped my comfort to socialize and communicate with others. It left me in a shell finding it difficult to leave the protection and comfort of aloneness. I would visit my in-laws and be quiet, not my usual chatty self. I am quieter at my own mixed family gatherings than I used to be. My spontaneity and lively spiritedness were "MIA." They are slow as the "DSL turtle" returning to what is now normal. It is going to be a long process. After all, it didn't take an hour to get to this state. It was 7 years in the making. It will take all of that, and perhaps more, to acclimate to what is termed "new normal."

I still struggle with opening that shell and coming out with my in-laws and family. I do not know if I will ever achieve the comfort level I once had. I feel so changed. I wish to be included, accepted and loved again by my family. We have all forever been changed by HD. It is difficult for me knock on the door not knowing if anyone is on the other side to open it. "Step by Step" as a dear friend says.

It is not until after HD, as in the case of my family, that a sense of order is re-established. (Our family hierarchy) Life as we know it, because of HD, is forever changed and must continue.

I needed to re-learn entry into this new life of unknowns and I'm getting there. I'm stepping out and helping others. I'm learning to stretch my wings and approach people to converse. It was a big step out of this created shell and comfort zone. It is not only an honor to hear other's stories. It is humbling to be in the presence of others and listen to their own journeys.

New Day Training and Bereavement Group

A funny thing happened to me one day when I was leaving church. It sounds like the preamble to an old Rodney Dangerfield joke except it is not. A wonderful nun made a "suggestion". I find it hard to say no to a nun. In my case, one that is as kind, loving and persuasive as this one. *I think they receive intense training in the art of persuasion.* I listened to her suggestion and a new door opened. Knowing of the recent death of my husband, this nun suggested that I get trained in a bereavement program called "New Day". She had hoped I would facilitate a bereavement group at our church with her and another parishioner. I was trained only a month and a half after Perry's death as a "Minister of Consolation".

I was trained by the creator of the program, Sr. Mauryeen O'Brien O.P. Sr. Mauryeen soon became not only my trainer; she became my mentor in working with the bereaved.

As I complete the writing of this book, I have begun my 7th seasonal year in facilitating the New Day program at our church. During the last 6 years I have evolved, thanks to Sr. Mauryeen, into a facilitator trainer of the New Day program and workshop presenter.

Another "Calling"

Amazing things occur with a little help from God above "if" you allow them to. Yes, this is another example of "Letting go and Letting God". It was an honor to be chosen to facilitate this program and be in the humble presence of the bereaved. This opened my spirit to another calling and another sign from Perry. It was nearing the first anniversary of his death as I sat co-facilitating the bereavement group at church. Then "it" happened. It was a calling as strong as the one I received when it was time for parenthood. This calling was a future in working with the bereaved.

The Anniversary Ritual

It strikes me as inappropriate to say that I "celebrate" the anniversary of Perry's death. At death, we celebrated his life. When reminiscing, we also celebrate the life he lived. Instead, I will say that I acknowledge it. Every year marks the passage of time. It is the time that he has been gone from my physical presence, not my spiritual awareness.

On the first anniversary of his death, I acknowledged it with a ritual that gave me an answer. I watched the clock intently and went out to my back deck a few minutes before the time "I" noted he died in my arms. It was cold yet my face was warmed by the late February sun through a cloudy sky. I prayed to the heavens reflecting and thanking for the guidance of the year passed. I wrote a few notes in a special anniversary journal. And I wept. The weeping turned into full blown crying. I cried so hard that my stomach ached. My eyes were so full of tears that I could barely see in this moment of private grieving. As the exact time of death struck, a strong chilling wind howled through the leafless winter trees creating a dance like sway in the back yard. As that moment in time passed, I was able to regroup.

I repeat this ritual every year on the calendar date and time of his death. It is part of my healing process.

I guess this was the Divine signaling the "winds of change". It was a sign for me to go forth with my life and do what I am guided to do. I was to fulfill that future in working with the bereaved. This required a reinvention of self.

Every February within a couple weeks before the "anniversary" I get off balance. I am weepier and more sensitive. It is my body feeling the anticipation of the next mark in passage of time. Once the time of the death on that date passes, I am able to regroup and move forward. It is a weird phenomenon. I've learned not to question it and go with the flow.

Back To School

That reinvention required that I go back to college and further my education. I already have one bachelor's and one master's degree. They were connected with my old life, my police life and not this new one.

I returned to school with a mission in mind. Life began at "50" because that's when my reinvention started. I wanted to add certifications that weaved together my police and personal life experiences. I wanted to treat individuals, couples and families experiencing depression, anxiety, caregiving, trauma, loss, grief, bereavement, long term, chronic progressive, terminal illnesses, and lifecycle changes. My road as a marriage and family therapist and grief counselor/therapist was the path to follow.

The mission was accomplished through intense hard work, dedication, the addition of 17 extra pounds, and bunch of new tinsel on my scalp (gray hairs). I earned a Master of Family Therapy Degree (MFT) and subsequent certifications as a Certified Clinical Trauma Professional (CCTP) and Certified in Thanatology: Death, Dying and Bereavement (CT). I am so proud of these personal/professional achievements and now the ability to go forth and work with those in need of my services.

Support Is Available

My reinvention opened me to become involved in support groups for caregivers of HD and families with HD. These are available through local HDSA Chapters or Affiliates. (HDSA.org)

Bereavement support is also widespread. My involvement with "New Day continues" and I have recently helped out with another local bereavement group. All it took was a phone call to connect with them. Thanks to my colleagues Wendy and Rose-Marie, I facilitate a bereavement group whose parents lost their children to substance abuse. These are the supports I can now offer in my new profession.

It Still Hurts 6.5 Years Later

I am sure you have heard it a million times from someone, "you'll get over it." Get over what? Get over the death of your husband, your mother, your father, your child, your friend, your pet, your loved one. " Get Over?" One does NOT get over, the death of a loved one. One learns to live with the loss. I have accepted my loss, experienced and still experience pain of the grief at different times and different levels. I have adjusted to a world without him and remain connected with him in my own way as I move forward. I have learned to live with the loss of my husband.

I think it took about 3.5 years before I started feeling better. It was and is a multifaceted process because the foundation is LOVE. Some grief experts currently say the "average" can be up to 5 years. I think it is because I did so much grieving during the progression of HD. That is me. And everyone is different.

Everyone grieves differently and for a different period of time. Grief is not a cookie cutter reaction to a death. It is very personal and has many variables. The relationship you had with the deceased and the nature of their death are two such variables. I will end that here because this is not a book on grief.

I still cry when I think of him. It is not as often as in the beginning. Anniversaries, birthdays and special occasions bring emotions bubbling from inside. It becomes like the children's volcano science project. I am the volcano filled with baking soda (emotions). The occasion is vinegar. Once the vinegar is added to me I begin to bubble up from the inside. Instead of spewing a bubbling mess, I become a teary crying mess.

In my dining room hangs a large portrait of the four of us. It was taken one month after our adoption. We were a whole family. I often look at that and fondly remember the way we were at the beginning of our new "AffaiR. And with great pride, I reflect on the growth and progress of our now adult children. And I know Perry is equally proud of them as he watches over all of us.

What has helped my moments of grief after Perry's death through today are the continuous "signs" or after death communications I receive. No matter what anyone else thinks or says, they give me great comfort. People have reacted by shaking their heads or laughing in disbelief when I share them. The only people that understand are those that have lost a loved one as well. These signs provide me with a continuing bond to a love not lost, but a love gone only from "my" sight. Like the breath that leaves my lips as I speak, even in the cold air when I "see" it, gone only from my sight. Its existence, like my love remains in the depth of my heart and soul, only felt by me.

It Still Hurts Even 16 Years Later

It's been 16 years, and we have all grown and changed. There are few updates in the original book because it is now 10 years since I first published it. We have had no choice but to move forward as time has not stood still, we are not stuck in the past, only to remember fondly what we had and to grow from it. The portrait in our dining room has been taken down. We are no longer the family that was presented in that portrait. I have a smaller one that hangs in my office. The memory no longer has to be larger than life because that life was who we were and a building block into who we are. I recently perused photos from his last days in 2008 and his funeral. My eyes became a gushing waterfall of tears as if it was just 16 years ago. LOVE hasn't been erased from my heart or mind. Life became a multispeed treadmill that keeps me going. Sometimes fast, sometimes slow, most of the time at a pace I can handle.

My life is traveling in DRIVE, NOT REVERSE. Occasionally I may idle in NEUTRAL position or PARK for a spell to rest and reflect. I try to live life focused on the big picture, the windshield that is in front of me. That small rear-view mirror is there for a reason, to reflect back, to glance at, not to lose my focus on what is ahead. It is what lies ahead that is my destiny. Taking all that I have and am about to learn along the way.

-14-

The Blame Game

There is a list of things I have to blame on HD. It is because of HD certain things happened in my life. Believe it or not, the items on the list are not all bad. After you read my list, what could you imagine putting on yours?

Because of HD.......

- I fell head over heels in love.
- I married that love of "MY life"
- I traveled with the love of my life.
- I became a mom.
- I learned to love, live and survive a devastating illness.
- I crashed and burned.
- I learned I am only a human.
- I learned what it was like to truly CARE for the one you love.
- I lived in the "trenches of caregiving" during my husband's bat tle with HD.
- I learned to love and be intimate during an incurable illness.
- I watched the love of my life slowly slip away.

- I held death in my hands and watched a trapped spirit break free after death.
- I am seeing progress for caregivers in support groups.
- I learned about family systems.
- I learned that I am NOT a superwoman.
- I am a therapist & grief counselor.
- I am a widow & single mother and as such, I continue to struggle.
- I am a spouse survivor of HD.
- I have a purpose.
- I am involved with HDSA.
- I am honoring my husband's legacy.
- I still care.
- I am the HDSA CT-Affiliate Support Group Leader.
- I am inspired by other HD families.
- I was able to attend the 29th HDSA Convention in Kentucky 2014.
- I was surrounded by LOVE and felt LOVE at the Convention.
- I was honored and blessed to meet other families on their journeys of hope, love and the quest for treatment and cure for HD.
- I am sharing my LOVE with all the families that are touched by this book

-15-

H.D.S.A. Revisited

Renewed Involvement With The HD Community

The evolution of my involvement with HD began in early 1978. Perry and I supported his father in Hartford, CT at a fundraising basketball game for HD. We made a white canvas banner with the current HD logo and border in blue felt. Marjorie Guthrie was present and spoke in behalf of what was then the Committee to Combat Huntington's Disease. And Dad made an "outstanding" speech at the fundraiser.

My next chapter involving HD was when I attended a HD support group at the UCONN Health Center. Bonnie was a newcomer to the UCONN HD program team in October 1999. In September 2000 she began facilitating monthly caregivers' support groups and continues to do so.

I do not remember when I attended the support group. I am thinking it was after Perry's horrific bike accident in October

2001 and before I crashed and burned from Caregiver Syndrome in October 2003.

I do remember I attended one and one was enough at the time. I sat amongst approximately 5-6 HD spouses. I listened to the stories of each person at that table. It upset me that I was the only spouse actually "living and caring for my HD loved one" at home. All the others present at that group had placed their spouses in nursing homes.

I did not return because I was not in the same league as they. I thought to myself, "how could they know what I was going through on a day-to-day basis in the trenches?" As I write this, I realize how narrow minded I was at the time, 11-13 years ago. I now realize that I knew NOTHING about the other spouse stories other than what I heard and processed at the time. I did not know if any of them had kept their loved one's home until they felt they "had to be moved" to a nursing home. I was blinded by the "nursing home" stigma. I promised my husband that I WOULD NOT place him in a nursing home, and I was going to keep my word, no matter what!

As I sit here and write, I realize I was very judgmental of the others. My God, how unfair I was in thinking that about other families! I said earlier that I am writing about how I perceived my life with HD. And I own up to this also. The more I think about it, it must have been after Perry got home in November 2001 and before I started my downward spiral into the deep stifling caregiver depression. After all, why did I need a caregiver support group when I was a "superwoman" and I was able to do it all? I know now that was a big mistake.

I returned to Bonnies' UCONN HD Caregiver Support Group in 2012. This time it was after I began facilitating/ leading support groups for the HDSA CT-Affiliate in Norwich, CT. This time I was nonjudgmental and open minded. This was after the fact because now I was a spouse survivor of HD. Now I have been through training as a Marriage and Family Therapist and understood more about the Family System.

It took me a decade to discover something. Over ten years later I saw how the support group evolved. I witnessed caregivers of HD with loved ones at home discuss their struggles. I heard reality. I heard what it was like to be in the trenches with HD struggling on a day-to-day basis. I saw how the support group evolved and was thankful and delighted it did. There are so many HD families that benefit from the UCONN group. We are very blessed to have their program, with Bonnie, available in Connecticut.

There is a big difference between the UCONN group and mine. The UCONN Team performs evaluations and a treatment plan. The medical staff is on the front line for clinical trials in CT and able to disseminate the information firsthand. Fortunately, they also bring the information to the HDSA-CT Affiliate Education Conference Days in keynote addresses.

The Huntington's Disease program at UCONN has evolved since our days of annual visits to their neurology department. At that time, we were told in an empathetic way year after year, the disease is progressing, your husband is doing better than we expected and there is still nothing we can do. It was done in a loving, caring, yet helpless way. There was no hope. The treatment was Haldol (the same medication Perry's mother was prescribed back in the 1980's). We were told to keep doing what we were doing. And see you again next year. We came to the conclusion that the kids gave Perry and me a purpose. Their life with us was the medication we needed that no one but they could provide.

There are now clinical trials and new FDA approved medications. There is speech therapy, physical therapy and swallowing tests. Thank goodness for modern research and medicine. Currently, there is no cure, but there is certainly progress being made since his diagnosis in 1992 and the HD gene identification in 1993.

2014 HDSA Connecticut Affiliate Education Conference

The HDSA-CT Affiliate sponsored an Education Conference on April 5, 2014. The headliner and anchor speakers made an incredible impact on me. One gave me hope for the future of HD families. The other put into words some of the symptoms of HD that I experienced as a caregiver.

Dr. Carolyn Drazinic: Changes 15-20 Years Before…..

The first speaker was Dr. Carolyn Drazinic. She has this long title of assistant professor in the Department of Psychiatry and the Department of Genetics and Developmental Biology at UCONN Health Center in Farmington, CT and a huge, impressive biography. With a marquee like that, I was expecting a brainiac doctor whose highly educated scientific talk would be dull as a doorknob. *Here I go with stereotyping and being judgmental.* Wrong again! In walked the warmest, kindest down to earth woman with bright eyes, a friendly smile and a sense of humor. A real person! She was a triple winning combination of brains, beauty and personality.

Dr. Drazinic used a lot of technical scientific jargon that did not penetrate my nonscientific brain. *(My two brothers inherited the scientific gene. That gene passed over me. I guess it must have been male dominant.)* One statement she made was that the brain changes in the person with HD are happening 15 to 20 years "before" symptom manifestation.

As I sat in the audience, I thought Perry would have been ages 13 to 18. Could it have been that by age 20 he already had some gut insight he would get HD, hence the reason for the young age vasectomy? We will never know. Something certainly dictated the way he chose to live and the choices he made along the way.

Dr. Drazinic gave names to 2 of the behaviors we experienced with HD. PERSERVATION, which I thought was his obsessive behavior. Perry would keep asking over and over again the same question or act obsessive having to order fishing gear with over-night shipping even though he did not need it for months. Apparently with HD, this is different than clinical OCD (obsessive compulsive disorder). The second was ANOSOGNOSIA, I understood this as lack of or impaired awareness of the disease. This lack of or impaired awareness becomes evident in the HD person's perception of motor, cognitive and emotional abilities.

I now had some insight, albeit, after the fact of what made Perry do some of the things he did. That's why driving, walking, running, and riding his bike was so hard to give up in the name of safety. No wonder why he seemed so oblivious of the changes that were occurring.

Of course, would what I have just learned now have helped me at the time we were going through it? My guess is probably not. At that time, we were trying to survive the slow progression of this knowingly fatal disease. There was no cure then and no cure now. The difference is that there is more scientific research and there are more clinical trials creating hope and at least some symptom management. That is a huge step in the right direction.

It was very emotional for me to hear Dr. Drazinic speak of her continued work on symptom management and the search for a cure for HD. I hope and pray for more progress in the scientific community to help HD families.

The anchor speaker was Jimmy Pollard. Jimmy is globally known for his involvement in the HD Community. He hails from our own New England backyard in Lowell, MA where he worked with people with HD for 26 years. He authored the book on HD, "Hurry Up and Wait". Most importantly, Jimmy is another friendly, caring, grounded, gentle, and a "Real McCoy" kind of person.

Jimmy spoke of a topic he calls the "Huntington's Disease Disguise". *(I am looking at my notes that I took during his segment. I surely hope I have done his talk justice.)* Just exactly what is the HD Disguise? He said it signals something different about a person. It is a "mask" that misconstrues what a person is thinking, it displays as a missed impression. And because of this, friends slowly vaporize. "Slowly Vaporize" is a powerful statement!

Yes, I saw this HD Disguise when I took pictures of Perry. It is evident in many photos of the disease's progression. I used to think that Perry was looking "through" me when I spoke to him. It was as I described earlier in this book when his beautiful blue mischief making, sparkling Caribbean blue topaz eyes changed to a look of emptiness. This HD Disguise gave Perry a very bland affect.

I think the bland affect of the HD Disguise coupled with his silence made friends uncomfortable. The progression of the disease was also a cause of his friend's vaporization. He was no longer the person they once knew. They also grieved when they saw what HD was doing to him. It was easier for them to stay away.

Jimmy was spot on *(after all he was the professional, I only the caregiver)* as he described five layered features of this disguise. He described a disorder of muscle tone and postural change as dystonia. I remember this occurring when Perry was sitting. I thought he was jittery and restless. Because of this, someone thought he was drunk or in distress as he sat in church during our nephews christening. They were ready to remove him until I spoke up.

Another layer he mentioned was motor impersistence. An example he gave for motor persistence is holding a cup; it is held with a contracture. Motor impersistence occurs when the person with HD is talking and holding a cup lets go, they are unable to maintain or persist in the holding contracture. This brought to mind Perry's dropping things like tools in the garage when he was tinkering with his motorcycle. He dropped glassware in the kitchen. We were well stocked in plastic cups and dishes from then on.

Next are general changes in posture. Jimmy described how postural changes occur in the face, such as shoulder drops, head drops, balance and spatial awareness. These are vivid to me because they too are frozen in time with photos. They became very evident after Perry's 2001 bicycle accident. That trauma created a whole host of changes that brought these HD layers to the surface.

Modulating force was another layer Jimmy described as rocking or lurching to get out of a chair. I knew when Perry was preparing to get up from a chair. I did not realize it was a process in HD. I think back at doing the count of "1, 2, 3, up" when I was trying to synchronize my timing with Perry in getting him out of the chair when he needed help. If it wasn't for that syncing, one or both of us would have ended up on the floor!

The last layer was slow processing creating delayed response. As HD progressed, I found it was easier and necessary to speak slower to Perry. It was a lesson in patience for me because life was like bees flying around a beehive. It was busy and quick with no pattern whatsoever. Slow and steady was not in the instruction manual at the time. I learned to be patient with not only me; I had to be more patient with Perry.

There is nothing better than learning something and being able to apply it to real life. Isn't that after all what we hope to do in college or after a training class? In the case of Jimmy Pollards presentation, I had already lived it. I just didn't know it had a name in our time.

All this new information is helping me realize that HD was poking its head out of the sand like a Whack A Mole game for many years. It would surface and go away, surface and go away, except, it never really "went" anywhere. Was it dormant at times or was it because I did not "see" it? During the years until 1994 we were childless. We did our own thing. We worked, and I worked different shifts including holidays and weekends. We really didn't have a "social life" with couples. We had friends. We both went to graduate school. We vacationed with and without each other. For the most part, life was good and stable when he wasn't involved in any accidents.

What DOES MATTER is that Predictive testing and embryo testing are available. NEW medications are being clinically tested and approved. Symptoms CAN be managed with medication. And new therapies ARE available. There is MORE support available than EVER before! There ARE active research studies in progress. AND because of all that HD now has new "labels" indicating earlier than diagnosis descriptions of behavior. These are ANSWERS!! THIS IS PROGRESS!! There is MORE HOPE than ever before. And there is still more to do.

Systemic Constellations, HD & Me

I had the privilege to be a workshop presenter in between the presentations of Dr. Drazinic and Jimmy Pollard at the 2014 HDSA Connecticut Affiliate Education Conference.

Another of my certifications is as facilitator in Systemic Constellations. I was trained in Constellations by my former MFT college professor and supervisor, J. Edward Lynch PhD. Ed is the founder and director of the New England Institute of Systemic Constellations. (systemicinstitute.com) His teachings are built upon the context of its founder, Bert Hellinger. I give this piece of history because it was in a book of Bert Hellinger's that I found a connection with Huntington's Disease. In his book, To the Heart of the Matter, Bert Hellinger included a brief therapy with Three Siblings entitled "We take you, with all that entails" Incurable genetic disease (Huntington's Chorea) (pages 46-52)

It was with this information that I presented a workshop at this HD education conference. Without getting too involved in the actual process, I will briefly explain what transpired. Four people were present at my workshop. It happened to be the precise number of people needed. Interestingly another person poked their head into the room and left. We had a father who was recently diagnosed with HD. We had representatives for his son, his future wife and his future child. I facilitated a carefully crafted and scripted dialogue of stem sentences to the representatives. The father was able to "get" from his "son" acceptance of all that HD entails at the full price that it costs both of them. It ended with a hug between the two. Tears between "father" and "son" were shed. The "son" then introduced his "wife" and "child" to his "father".

The "father" felt relief to hear the acceptance. He said his heart needed to hear it since he knew in his real world it is unlikely he would hear such words from his son. It was a powerful exercise wrapped in the emotion of a parent's guilt of potentially passing on this hereditary disease experience. I was honored to bring this gift to the family. And I was humbled to be in the presence of a room full of love, acceptance and inclusion. It was a beautiful experience.

-16-

The Perfect Place To Close An Imperfect Story

Louisville, KY 2014.

I attended the 29th Annual HDSA Convention in Louisville, KY this year as the CT-Affiliates Representative for Leadership Day. I came away with what is now the information for the final chapter in this book.

I had the honor and privilege to meet HD families, caregivers and friends of those with HD from across this great country. I witnessed interaction with adults with HD, children with HD, entire families, parents and children, extended family members and friends of those with HD. These are families who live generation to generation standing on the edge of the HD cliff. Some are At-Risk, some gene positive and others are symptomatic in varying stages.

I was able to put a face to names I've only seen in print on the HDSA.org website or Facebook. The Convention was kicked off by an HDSA Team Hope Walk along the Ohio Riverfront named the "Louisville Loop". We were a noisy group upon exiting our meeting place at the Galt House Hotel. We wore powder blue Team Hope Walk t-shirts. And we were adorned with handmade ornaments, noisemakers and posters.

We were "the" crowd to watch walking down the street. We were young, middle aged and old. We walked, gaited, and wheeled. We had "swagger", spirit and camaraderie. We were a "family" like no other. A family whose every member "got it". Everyone, yes, everyone who attended was included. There were no exclusions. This was an environment rich in hope, inspiration and to no surprise LOVE!

This Convention is like a family union of first comers like me. Without a doubt it was a "Reunion" of the extended HD family who had attended in the past. And as in many a reunion, we had our identifying apparel and accessories. We had HD Convention tote bags, lanyards and t-shirts.

Probably one of the most inspiring things I saw was a street front banner that said, "Louisville, Its Possible Here!" That was no mistake. I have learned through my systemic constellations training that the knowing field is just that. Louisville "knew" that we were a very special group, and things were possible. I was witness to things at the convention that I did not think possible.

My "It" would have to be the inspiration I got from the people I met and the stories they told. My "It" is definitely Love; New Friends and Colleagues in a place where everyone in this HD family could gather and feel they belonged.

LOVE Beyond Words.

Just picture this if you could: shoulder rubs, hand holding, pushing the wheelchair, adjusting the brake on the rollator, the hand on the back of a loved one as their arms flail with chorea, the arm reached around the loved one gently caressing the far shoulder during the "Hope not Hype" presentation, the couple sitting "connected" to each other shoulder to arm in contact and each other's presence felt.

The Last Dance

The last event of the Convention was a dinner gala. It was a dinner dance for all to participate. What I witnessed became the best place to close this chapter. After dinner, the music filled the room. People entered the dance floor filled with joy. The true sense of camaraderie was to see the doctors, the researchers and the HDSA staff take to the dance floor. They joined and blended with the kids, adults and families. Everyone was "one".

No one cared who jerked, gaited, missed a step, couldn't step, and surprisingly no "twerking". Music is magic and it took place on that dance floor.

"Tonight's gonna be a good night" was an earlier theme song. It spoke volumes as I observed a man pull his almost limp honey out of her wheelchair and hold her tight on that dance floor. She could not move; she hung like a marionette whose strings were cut. That didn't matter to him because at that moment, that very moment they were a "couple" on that dance floor purely enjoying the music. My eyes welled as I took notes to enter into this book. Another husband held his unsteady wife while dancing and "no one" was out of place. Then there was a woman who picked up a man out of a wheelchair. He was unsteady yet able to stand and muster a box step type move. She was so happy to see him up. The smile on his face was of great joy. After the song they wheeled by me, and I complimented them on how beautiful they were. She proudly smiled and said, "This is my brother!"

My mind was shouting: Hold Me! Guide Me! Be With Me! I am here with you! I am holding onto you! I am holding you up and will not let you go! I have you! In a moment of solace I wondered, what would it have been like, if Perry and I had a "last dance" like that. I can tell you it would have been extremely dif- ficult because he was nearly a foot taller than me. There is no way on earth I could have picked him up and held him. We both would have fallen to the floor making room for what would've looked like break dancing about to begin.

The night was over. To me the event was a sweet success. To my mushy heart, it was a night to remember.

Without a doubt, it was:

An AffaiЯ Worth Remembering
With Huntington's Disease.

Incurable Love & Intimacy
During an Incurable Illness

Isn't Love beautiful?
Peace, *Debbie*

APPENDIX:

I.

Fast Facts on Huntington's Disease (HD)

The Huntington's Disease Society of America (HDSA) published a fast facts brochure in 2013.

What is Huntington's Disease?

Huntington's Disease (HD) is an inherited brain disorder that results in the progressive loss of both mental faculties and physical control. Symptoms usually appear between the ages of 30 to 50, and worsen over a 10 to 25 year period. Ultimately, the weakened individual succumbs to pneumonia, heart failure or other complications.

Everyone has the HD gene, but it is those individuals that inherit the expansion of the gene who will develop HD and perhaps pass it onto each of their children.

Presently, there is no effective treatment or cure. Although medications can relieve some symptoms, research has yet to find a means of slowing the deadly progression of HD.

Current estimates are that 1 in every 10,000 Americans has HD and more than 250,000 others are at-risk of having inherited it from a parent. Once thought a rare disease, HD is now considered one of the more common hereditary diseases. (HDSA, 2013)

Symptoms Include:
- Personality changes, mood swings and depression
- Forgetfulness and impaired judgment
- Unsteady gait and involuntary movements
- Slurred speech and difficulty in swallowing.

The Scope of HD

Approximately 30,000 Americans have HD, but the devastating effects of the disease touch many more.

Within a family, multiple generations may have inherited the disease. Those at-risk may experience tremendous stress from the uncertainty and sense of responsibility.

In the community, lack of knowledge about HD may keep friends and neighbors from offering social and emotional support to the family, fostering unnecessary isolation.

The Huntington's Disease Society of America (HDSA) has a nationwide network that provides support and referrals for individuals with HD and their families.

II.

The 6 Essentials to Pack for the HD Caregiver's Journey:

When we embark on a journey, we pack the essentials. These are the very basic "go-to" items in our "carry on" luggage. Here we will be packing six essentials. They will help you while caregiving a loved one with Huntington's Disease. Caregiving a loved one with Huntington's Disease is a journey. Throughout your caregiving journey, your own "carry on" piece will expand. It will grow to receive the limitless ideas and possibilities you add as your own "go-to" items. I encourage you to add your own "go-to" items to your "carry on" and share them with others embarking on this journey with Huntington's Disease.

1. Patience. As we've been told, the journey with Huntington's Disease is a long one. We need a lot of patience as we accompany our loved one through the changes and stages of HD. Most of all, we need patience with ourselves while enduring a life forever changed. Find your own comfortable pace in this marathon.

2. Humility. "I cannot do this alone". A humble person knows, is aware of, and realizes their limitations. It takes courage and great inner strength to break the silent suffering of going it alone. A humble person knows it is okay to ask for help. All you have to do is ask. With a little help, your luggage will be lighter to carry on this journey.

3. Food, Tea, and a Blanket. Being a caregiver is tiring. For the long journey with HD, we need sustenance for our own mind, body and soul. Self-care is key. We need a healthy diet and know when to rest our mind and bodies. We may brew a cup of favorite tea, have a snack, wrap up in a warm blanket, lose ourselves in a good book and just **be**. Taking a Personal Time Out (PTO) to recharge our batteries on a regular basis helps keep us strong to continue on this journey with HD and our loved one.

4. A Doodle Pad. Using a doodle pad, a journal, or any type of media, jot down or draw your feelings without judging them. Use any creative constructive outlet to let them out. We are human and have feelings that we cannot control. We can however, control the way we express them in a healthy and safe way. Caregiving a loved one with HD and its journey is fertile ground for a variety of feelings. Give your feelings constructive expression and let them flow. It is a great release.

5. Forgiveness. We need to find any extra weight in our "carry on" that is slowing us down and "LET GO" of it. It is that stuff that won't help us on this journey. Bitterness and resentment are two "weights" we sometimes carry as caregivers. Forgiveness lightens our heart. Accepting the reality of life with HD and living one day at a time allows us to focus on what we can do. Forgiveness allows us to carry on in the present being available for every precious moment.

6. Humor. We need to laugh on this journey at ourselves and with our loved ones. Laughter is a great release. Humor helps us survive. I remember a time I put the toaster in the refrigerator. It was no wonder that I could not find it in the pantry! I was a caregiver and clearly it was time for a break. Yes, I laughed at myself. Can you remember a laughable moment?

Please make copies of this packing list and share it with anyone you know who is on the journey as a caregiver with Huntington's Disease. Sharing knowledge and tips are gifts of love from one caregiver to another. Through sharing, we learn that we are not alone on this journey with HD.

Supporting you in this HD Journey,

Debbie

Modified from: Packing for the Grief Journey: Six Essential Items by my colleague, Cheryl Amari, M.A., CT., GriefTeach.com. (This was a workshop I presented at the: 2014 HDSA CT Affiliate Education Conference.)

Resources used for this book:

Amari,C. M.A.,CT., GriefTeach.com.

Hellinger, B. *To the Heart of the Matter.* Heidelberg, Germany: Carl-Auer-Systeme, 2003.

Huntington's Disease Society of America
     505 Eighth Avenue
     New York, NY 10018
     HDSA.org
          Law Enforcement Tool Kit
          Caregiver Law Enforcement Tool Kit
          Fast Facts about HD

MerriamWebster.com. 2014

O'Brien, Mauryeen O.P. *The New Day Journal. A journey from grief to healing. For people coping with the loss of a loved one:* Skokie, IL, 2000.

UCONN Health Center- Huntington's Disease Program
     263 Farmington Avenue
     Farmington, CT 06030
     UCHC.edu

About the Author: 2014
Debbie Pausig, MFT, CT, CCTP

HDSA-CT Affiliate support group leader and conference presenter, Marriage and Family Therapist (MFT) having earned a Master's in Marriage and Family Therapy from Southern CT State University.

Certified in Thanatology (CT) Death, Dying and Bereavement with ADEC (Association for Death Education and Counseling)

Certified Clinical Trauma Professional (CCTP) with IATP. (International Association of Trauma Professionals)

Certified Facilitator in Systemic Constellations through the New England Institute of Systemic Constellations.

Minister of Consolation/Bereavement Facilitator & Trainer through the Family Life Office-Archdiocese of Hartford, CT

Bereavement Facilitator with the Newtown Parent Connection, Newtown, CT

Develops and offers workshops on grief and has recently developed and conducted a workshop to assist bereavement facilitators who may become affected by the losses presented to them in their groups.

25-year veteran of the North Haven Police Department, North Haven, CT having earned a Bachelor's in Law Enforcement and Master's in Public Administration from the University of New Haven, CT.

She combines her professional experience with the personal experience of being a caregiver, widow and "spouse survivor" of HD.

Her husband Perry, died with HD in 2008 at age 50 after living with its progression for 17 years. She and Perry adopted their children, Katherine and Daniel, in 1994.

Debbie is a "systems" trained therapist. She pursued this training as a direct result from living with HD which affects the "family system".

ALSO, BY DEBBIE PAUSIG
New in 2024

The "Freshman 15 16" of Grief
Losing My Forever Love & Finding My Way

Ten years ago, Debbie Pausig took a chance and self-published her first book, *"An AffaiЯ Worth Remembering With Huntington's Disease, Incurable Love & Intimacy During an Incurable Illness."* It was where she took us through the caregiver's journey of her love story entangled with the incurable neurological disorder, Huntington's Disease. It was a journey many caregivers related to, no matter what the disease, because it is all about LOVE.

The "Freshman 15 16" of Grief begins when Huntington's Disease took the life of her husband and now reaches a larger audience. Debbie extends out to those who have not only lost a spouse through death. The journey traverses' other losses and growths during the mid-life + aging process that have occurred in the 16 years after the death of her forever love. This is a time that is full of both expected and unexpected changes: Widowhood, single parenthood, returning to school, unemployment, pet loss, career reinvention, menopause, becoming an adult orphan, relocation, adult children, travel, fun, learning, gratitude, friendships and the general aging process to the Medicare age of 65. That is the progression of her life.

Real and raw, sad, and humorous, this book validates the power and resilience of the human spirit. And the grace and mercy that God bestows on us as we learn to live without those loved ones who have died. And the ability to adapt to the constant changes in life.

Debbie lives in North Haven, CT having raised her two children, Kate, and Daniel, after the 2008 death of her husband, Perry from Huntington's Disease.

Cover Design by Nina Ciarleglio